THE HORSES OF THE NEW DAWN

Origins of The Horses Know Trilogy

LYNN MANN

Coxstone Press

Copyright © 2025 by Lynn Mann

Lynn Mann asserts the moral right to
be identified as the author of this work.

Paperback ISBN 978-1-7393276-6-8
Hardback ISBN 978-1-7393276-7-5
Published by Coxstone Press 2025

All rights reserved.

No part of this book may be reproduced in any form or by any electronic or mechanical means, including information storage and retrieval systems, without written permission from the author, except for the use of brief quotations in a book review.

This novel is entirely a work of fiction. The names, characters and incidents portrayed in it are the work of the author's imagination. Any resemblance to actual persons, living or dead, events or localities is entirely coincidental.

This book was created without the use of Artificial Intelligence (AI). The use of any part of this book for AI training, machine learning, or any other similar purpose without prior written permission from the author is strictly prohibited.

You're always in my heart, Pie

Prologue

The forest whispers their names to me even though I know that much time will pass before the world is ready for them. When The Horses Of The New Dawn make their entrance, it will be because the human race is finally ready for change. Until then, the bonded horses of each generation will ensure that the humans avoid us, whilst supporting their progress as the forests support ours.

Laceheart of the Kindred

Chapter One

FAO: General Harris
FROM: Lieutenant Miller
SUBJECT: Summarised missive from forward scouts
The enemy is approximately two weeks' march away from our front lines. They match us in number, horses and light weaponry but have twice as many cannons.

PAIN PULSED in my feet and rippled up through my legs to my body, where it changed from the dull protest of overuse to the sharp pangs of hunger. My teeth rattled against my ribs as I swiped at a winged tormentor trying to draw my life fluid from its already depleted supply. I hobbled over to the vessel that occasionally provided relief from my thirst, only to find it empty.

I was aware of, and took comfort from, the noble intentions of those caring for me and the others of my kind, but their efforts weren't enough; I needed more fluid and nutrition than they could provide. My body was failing. But it could not – not yet. For he was near. I had waited so long for him and now, finally, he was near.

When a ripple had disturbed the misery of my existence, I immediately realised who had caused it. I sensed the power he unknowingly held inside of him, and what that would mean not only for him and me, but for all his kind and mine. I sensed his ability to see that which few other humans could. I sensed his courage in remaining true to himself regardless of the aggression his stance provoked in those around him. I sensed the soul with whom I resonated so closely, so deeply, that once we were together, we could never again be apart. The ripple had lifted me and given me strength, for it told me that both my wait and my misery would soon come to an end.

But he had not yet appeared. I could sense how close he was in proximity and yet how, as the days passed, his mind was failing and taking him further away from me. Where I had gained strength from knowing how close we were to meeting, thereby achieving my objective in this incarnation, he was weakening due to his belief that he had failed to achieve his.

His hungry, beaten body obeyed the drills to which it was subjected whilst his mind lashed relentlessly against itself, trying to work out what he had done wrong – how he could better have put across his argument against the violence in which he would now be forced to partake – whilst also trying to hold at bay the constant pummelling of fear and violence emanating from those around him. As a result, no matter how hard I tried, I couldn't reach him while he was awake. It was only when he slept that I could touch the mind sensitive enough to the energies around it to recognise them for what they were, and intelligent enough to know that they could never be allowed to prevail; it was only when he succumbed to an exhausted, dreamless slumber that I could soothe his gentle, beautiful mind with the energy of my heart, and slow its steady creep towards insanity.

So it was that, by the time I finally sensed his approach, the pathway between our minds was well established and merely waiting for him to recognise it.

He rounded the end stall of the hot, dusty, tormentor-infested barn in the company of a much better fed male whose arrogance and aggression only accentuated the lack of both in the thin, empty-eyed male in whom I had already placed my complete trust. The two humans stopped in front of my stall.

'Here you go, coward,' the larger male snarled, slamming his forelimb down on the top of the stall door. I flinched and stepped back out of his reach, as did those of my kind who stood in the stalls on either side of mine. 'This one's half dead by the look of it, so even you should be able to ride it. Training starts in the morning, eight o'clock sharp, so you'd best make a start on getting to know the nag who'll be carrying you into battle. Maybe then you'll have at least one friend before you end your craven existence, eh?' He slapped an implement for smoothing my coat into my destiny's forelimb and strode away.

The male whose body reflected his frail and abused mind sagged over the door, and I sensed him wondering whether now would be an appropriate time to give up on life completely. I shuffled forward and touched the top of his head. He stank of human cooling fluid, terror and hopelessness. I breathed into him my awareness of his intelligence, courage and integrity. I disturbed his hair with my nose, gently moving it in circles as my dam used to do whilst comforting me. I surrounded him with the energy of my heart.

He slowly raised his head and looked at me. His eyes roved over me from head to tail and back again, then he let out a long breath and slid the bolt across my stall door. He hobbled in beside me with the gait of a much older human, before turning to pull the door shut behind him. He felt about for the bolt but then hesitated as the energy of my heart reached his own.

He turned back to me, leaving the door unbolted. Where his eyes had been empty, they were beginning to brighten with the light of his soul. He lifted a trembling forelimb towards me but then quickly withdrew it and, dropping the grooming implement, rubbed it with his other forelimb as if I had bitten him. He screwed up his face even as his soul shone from his eyes with greater intensity.

I increased the flow of energy from my heart to his. He was as safe with me as I was with him. It mattered not that we were both battered in body and mind. We had found one another. All was well.

He lifted his shaking forelimb towards me again and this time laid it against my chest, at the exact place where the energy of my heart was emanating on its way to enfold his. I sensed his revulsion fading at the stench of the soiled earth of our stalls. The sounds of killing instruments clashing against one another on the training field no longer reached him as his heart slowed to beat in time with mine. His breathing slowed and deepened as I filled his vision to the exclusion of all else.

He moved his forelimb away from my chest with apparent difficulty and rubbed it up and down my neck. His voice was barely audible as he said, 'How is it that amongst all this horror, there's you? How is it that, all of a sudden, I feel safe, when we're both anything but?' He leant forward until his forehead rested against mine. 'You shouldn't be here. No horses should. This is our madness, not yours. I'm sorry I couldn't stop it. I'm so, so sorry.' Sadness flooded through him, and his shoulders shuddered.

I would ease his remorse. I would lift his spirit as his mere presence lifted mine. *Senses Balance you have no reason to feel sorrow. I am here in order to be with you.*

I felt his mind forming pockets of meaning from the energy I sent him. He stepped back from me, his eyes now flaring brightly even as his mind refused to accept that which it knew. 'That's it, I've finally gone mad,' he told himself. He put his forelimbs over his ears and shook his head, telling himself, 'I tried to fight it, I really tried, but it's all too much. It's got me.'

You are far from mad. You are merely sensitive to the energy that surrounds you. Including me.

He shook his head more firmly. 'No. I can't be hearing voices. I can't go insane near the horses; they've been through enough.'

He staggered towards the door, but I moved in front of it, knocking it ajar with my shoulder as I did so. He stumbled into me and only just put his forelimbs behind him in time to break his fall before landing on the soiled ground. He flung his forelimbs towards me. 'The door's open! Go! Go! Run away from me. From all this. Run far away until they stop chasing you, then never go anywhere near humans again.'

I stood where I was and held his eyes with mine so that our souls collided in an invisible explosion. His mouth fell open as droplets formed in his eyes and ran down his face.

Names are important to humans so I have named you for your ability. Senses Balance. You were never going to succeed in persuading others to see the truth this time around but that does not mean you have failed to achieve your purpose. In acting upon your ability with strength and integrity you have set yourself inexorably upon a path that will benefit us all.

He shook his head but did not tear his eyes from mine. Our souls would not allow it any more than they would allow his mind to continue its attempts at resistance.

So long as you keep your mind with mine you will survive until survival no longer serves us both, I told him.

He got to his feet and leant back against the slices of shade provider that made up the wall of my stall. He blinked many times as he explored the feeling of calm and safety afforded him by our newly established bond. When he spoke with his mind, I sensed a measure of stability returning to it. *Horses can't talk, but I'm hearing words in my head that I think are coming from you. How is that possible? And how is it that I believe it enough to think words back to you?*

You sense balance. You recognise that which takes you closer to it and that which pushes you further away. You have the courage to act upon that which you know. It is the reason your fellow humans despise you. They are not ready to accept that which is obvious to you. They will not be ready in this generation or indeed many to come.

Senses Balance's keen intelligence sifted through my assertions and made rapid sense of them. I knew what his question would be before he asked it. *How can I have set myself on a path that'll benefit us all if none of us will live long enough to see that benefit?*

We have never met and yet you know me. Explore the connection you feel with me and you will know the truth.

He blinked many more times before asking, *How can it be the truth when it doesn't make sense?*

You have been conditioned to believe that the life you are living is finite. Your body's existence is indeed so but the soul it carries is infinite. With your agreement we will find each other again when our souls next inhabit a body. When the time is right for you to continue to walk the path on which you have embarked with such tenacity. Once we are together again we will assist your kind and mine to evolve.

Chapter One

His speed at understanding and accepting our bond delighted me. *You have my agreement.* His mouth lifted at its corners even as he twisted his head from side to side.

I sensed his bewilderment at having readily agreed to a concept so foreign to his previous view of life. I shared his joy at our agreement, and at our bond as it filled his mind, pushing out his confusion until joy was all that dwelt there. Neither of us was disturbed from our rapture by the sounds of clashing, shouting and screaming nearby, the scents of human cooling fluid, life fluid and terror, or the feelings of fear, aggression and hopelessness.

I had to warn him though, of the challenge we would face. My heart beat more strongly so that its energy surrounded and pervaded him with greater intensity, my desire to soothe and protect him as strong as if he were my offspring. *It is not time for us to leave this incarnation just yet for there is more we must do. You have done well to accept and immerse yourself in our bond so readily but it will not be so easy to remain immersed when you are subjected more directly to the fears and insecurities of those around you. Our connection is strong but we are two surrounded by multitudes who believe firmly in falsehood over truth. Now that you have experienced relief from everything that has assaulted your mind you will find it difficult when that relief is challenged. When you feel as if you are being pulled away from our bond you should focus on the part of your mind where you will always find me.*

And if that doesn't work? A bolt of fear penetrated his calm.

When you are reduced to thinking rather than feeling then you should focus upon this. I showed him an image in his mind of one of my kind. Her coat was white and black instead of my grey, and she was shorter than I. Her tail shone so white it appeared silver, in contrast to the dirty white of mine with its streaks of black and grey. Her eyes were the colour of the expanse above us, where mine were the same colour as the rest of my kind who were standing in the surrounding stalls. We couldn't have appeared more different in body, but in soul we were the same.

'It's you.' He spoke out loud, but using his breath rather than his voice. 'How can that be? How can it be you when you're standing right here?'

Hers is the body that I will inhabit in our next incarnation together. When your mind cannot find me then let it see her. Let her be a reminder that our suffering in this incarnation will not continue for much longer. That she will be waiting for you when it is over.

Chapter Two

FAO: General Harris
FROM: Lieutenant Miller
SUBJECT: Private Appleyard
Sergeant Bolton has moulded the subject into a soldier who will obey orders despite his continued lack of courage and conviction. It has been noted, however, that he has become more vocal about his beliefs since beginning his training with the cavalry. I recommend his platoon join the first charge in order that his attempts to spread discord are silenced at the earliest opportunity.

WE TRAINED TOGETHER, my Bond-Partner and I, obeying without argument the instructions issued by those who claimed dominance over us. But while they wanted us totally committed to becoming a lethal weapon of destruction, with teeth primed to tear at flesh, hooves ready to thrash and crush, and sharp implements held aloft in promise, we were anything but. Each time Senses Balance sat astride my back, he was with me in mind, body and soul, and the ability for which I named him steadily intensified. Even as our bodies continued to weaken, our bond only strengthened, to the extent that by the time we were informed we were ready for battle, I was confident that Senses Balance would easily recognise it when next we met in the flesh.

They mean for us to die, Senses Balance told me as I walked behind a female of my kind carrying a male human dressed in clothes identical to those of my rider. *"Cannon fodder", the captain called us. If we follow orders and charge when the sergeant orders it, then apparently, we'll die an honourable death. If we turn and run, we'll be caught and hanged as cowards. The captain looked at me when he said that. He thinks that just because I tried to stop this pointless, senseless war, that makes me craven.*

I knew everything he was telling me – I was with him in his mind when he and his fellow soldiers were being told the order of their final day – but I allowed him to continue without letting him know that was the case. He would never be able to reconcile why humans were so intent on killing one another, why he hadn't been able to persuade those who had control over the rest that there was a way to maintain peace, or why one of the males considered superior to him would not only waste lives as carelessly as he was apparently intent on doing, but tell those he was sending to their deaths that they were merely a means to exhaust their enemy's supply of cannon balls so that "better men" than Senses Balance could reach and kill them. He was too far ahead of them in outlook to be able to reconcile any of that. But in telling me about the events that had led to our final day and his feelings about it all, his bitterness gradually changed to sadness, so that as we took our place in line, facing the humans we were told were our "enemy",

Chapter Two

he was at least reconciled with how we would be leaving this incarnation.

Together, he affirmed as much to himself as to me.

Together, I agreed.

There was movement to one side of us as one of my kind was forced, with sharp implements attached to her rider's hind limbs, between me and she whom I had followed to the battleground.

'Ready for this, craven?' the newly arrived rider asked Senses Balance. My Bond-Partner's shudder rippled through me at the insanity he could feel rolling off his inquisitor, who continued, 'I'll be riding alongside you because believe me, nothing will give me more pleasure than to take your head from your shoulders if you show even the first sign of not keeping up, or of turning and running. There'll be no trial for you, no chance to spout any more of your crap before they hang the life out of you – oh no, I have very specific orders where you're concerned. You'll die with the rest of us, so that better men can live, or I'll see your head ground into the earth before I go to my maker.' The male showed all of his teeth at the thought.

Senses Balance took a deep breath and replied with a calm strength. 'My name is John Appleyard, and I am indeed ready to die in the mad charge you think you're forcing me to be a part of – not because I'm scared of you, but because my horse and I have chosen this day to leave all this insanity behind and embrace who we really are.'

I sensed rage permeating the other male's madness and felt his body priming itself for more of the violence he had routinely unleashed upon Senses Balance. I also sensed nearby riders – whose mounts had been sure to keep them within range of my partner's influence during training as well as now – taking comfort from his words. His courage infused them and stilled their terror. His sincerity pierced their self-deception and reassured them with the truth. The energy of his heart, emanating strongly from him as he spoke of me, gave them the strength to embrace the end of their nightmare.

My heart beat strongly with the energy in which I enfolded my rider, protecting and fortifying him even as he did the same for me. We knew who we were and who we would be. We were strong in mind, if weak in body. Immersed in our bond, we waited for the blows that would surely rain down upon us from the lunatic beside us.

'Sergeants, begin the charge,' roared a voice from behind us.

The enraged male satisfied himself with landing a single blow to Senses Balance's head before bellowing, 'Platoon, walk forward. Prepare to charge.' Madness was now the whole of him. A lifetime of fear – of his sire; of males with whom he had been imprisoned; at the realisation of his fate once he joined the fighting force; and now at the prospect of imminent death – had tumbled in on itself and left him unaware of anything other than the violence and aggression which he saw as his sanctuary.

I couldn't have been more gratified that Senses Balance continued to focus exclusively upon me. He didn't hear the whimpers and moans of other humans in the line. He didn't scent their excrement. He sat calmly astride my back, his heart beating with mine, as he waited for his next order. He was everything I had known he would be.

'Draw your swords!'

Senses Balance sighed as he obeyed.

'Hold the line! Charge!' The mad human's voice cracked as he uttered his last word. He stank of newly emitted body fluids of all kinds as his weary mount galloped painfully alongside me, and he shrieked louder than anyone when loud bangs reached us shortly before missiles penetrated our bodies.

The pain that tore through me was amplified by that afflicting my Bond-Partner. Despite his agony, he wrapped his forelimbs around my neck as all four of my limbs faltered, determined that his body would remain with mine after we hit the ground. His efforts were in vain, and he was flung a short distance away from me as my hind end overtook my head, and I landed on my back. My kind galloped over and past us, driven harshly forward by riders of other platoons, many of whom had convinced themselves that if they could just reach their "enemy", they might survive. All of them were torn from their bodies by those whom they perceived as separate from them.

I allowed the ridiculousness of such a concept to flow through me, as I had on every other occasion that I had been confronted with it, and focused on enfolding Senses Balance with the energy of my heart for as long as I could keep it beating. I would protect him from the viciousness of our surroundings as much as I could, for as long as I could.

He crawled towards me, life fluid pulsing from his chest with as much force as it did from mine. He lay down in the warm pool I was creating even as it disappeared into the cracks of the hard, dry ground, taking my body's life force with it. He put his forelimb across my neck, rested his head upon mine and breathed out a wet, gurgling sigh.

I never named you. His communication was as impassioned as his body was frail. *They called you "Dusty", but that wasn't your name; I knew it wasn't, but I just couldn't seem to think of a better one. I have it now though. Angel. That's who and what you are. You saved me, my Angel, and I can't thank you enough.*

I sent him as much of my heart energy as I could with its last beat, hoping it would be enough to remind him of my devotion to him and give him the strength to let go of his body, rather than fight death as were most of his compatriots. I left my body easily, gratefully, and waited... but not for long. Senses Balance welcomed the energy of my heart and allowed it to enfold him as he relinquished his grip on life. I sensed him reaffirming to himself everything we had agreed to do in our next incarnation.

Next time, he told me.

Next time, I agreed.

We left it all behind.

Chapter Three

FAO: General Harris
FROM: Lieutenant Miller
SUBJECT: Casualties
Following reports from the medics, I can confirm that there were no survivors from our first charge. None of our men reached the enemy's front line, but estimates suggest that a significant proportion of their ammunition was used in ensuring that was the case. I have concluded that the first charge was a success.

HE SOON BECAME DISORIENTATED. Confused. Overwhelmed by the trauma of his last months as John Appleyard. Now that he had no body, no brain to slow his thoughts or process his emotions, he felt them all simultaneously and intensely – disappointment, frustration, rage, hopelessness, sadness and terror. He attempted to flee from his pain; from everything about his incarnation, including me.

Senses Balance. I can help you.

He perceived me as being in front of him even though he thought he had left me behind. His anguish kept him from the realisation that there was nowhere to go, for he was everywhere and everything, including me. He convinced himself that he turned away from me and everything of which I reminded him, and fled once more. The speed with which he believed he accomplished both surprised and bolstered his effort.

Senses Balance. My use of his name once more revealed to him his mistake. The energy of my heart was more powerful than all the emotions to which he believed he was captive, and the fact that I no longer incarnated a physical heart rendered it even more so. I surrounded him and immersed myself in him. We were one and always would be.

His fear beat a slow but spiky rhythm as it wound through the rest of his energy, preventing him from consolidating his courage and strength. His hopelessness and sadness weighed heavily and stopped him from recognising his light. His anger burned so fiercely that he continually recoiled from himself.

When his rage flared at me, I refused to retreat. Its repeated attempts to burn me failed and, in fact, cooled with each attempt until it merged with the part of him that was benign. When his fear would separate him from me, I compressed it until its spikes were no more. I lifted his sadness and hopelessness until his light shone through underneath, obliterating his darkness.

Senses Balance remembered who I was to him and quickly relaxed into his new situation as only a soul as practised as his could. *Angel. You're still helping me here in the oneness, as you did in the physical. Thank you.* His gratitude flowed throughout my being with ferocity.

In truth you needed little help. You have made the transition between life and death more times than most and are processing this one rapidly.

Senses Balance was true to his name. *But there's more to process, I can feel it. Can you help me do it, the way you just did with the other stuff?*

I merely responded to the aspects of your energy that you had grown into the habit of directing towards those around you. That which remains is that which you direct towards yourself.

He instantly identified the disappointment and frustration pervading his soul at his inability to express himself with confidence when it had mattered. Anguish became all of him as he relived again all the meetings he had sat through with those with whom he felt he should have been articulate enough, persuasive enough, confident enough, to persuade to follow his advice, so that war could have been avoided; as he remembered that millions would have suffered due to his perceived inadequacy; as he remembered the agony of his and my deaths, and the scents and sounds as so many lay dying around us. His anguish became a desperation to atone for his perceived shortcomings that tore through us both.

The energy of my heart flared brightly, smoothing out his emotions once again, so that his experience from processing so many previous incarnations could once more come to his rescue. He arrived at the answer to his predicament without need of further assistance from me.

We agreed to incarnate again together when we can help humans and horses to evolve, he affirmed. *My next incarnation will give me the opportunity to be everything I could not be in my last one.*

Something in his statement vibrated with a different energy from the rest – something that he had yet to fully understand. He repeated it to himself. *We can help horses to evolve.* He directed his attention towards me and instantly gained the understanding he sought. *It isn't just me who needs to incarnate in order to release that which is trapped within my soul. You do too. And when we do it, we'll be showing all the others how to do it too.*

His realisation brought his deliberating to a conclusion. He released the humanity to which he had clung during the entirety of his incarnation despite extreme provocation, and with it, its inevitable worries and fears about the task upon which we had agreed.

He celebrated his oneness with All That Is as he remembered that which incarnating as a human had caused him to forget – that he had never been apart from it. I celebrated with him even though my choice to incarnate as one with four limbs had ensured my awareness of the truth had remained intact. I swirled with him as he did the energetic equivalent of a leap for joy. I rejoiced with him as we touched other souls with whom he and I had incarnated, both this time and in many other lifetimes. Through it all, I fuelled the spark of impatience I sensed within him to incarnate again, by recognising the same spark within my own soul. We were one with the swirling consciousness of souls, and yet we singled ourselves out with our shared sense of determination and excitement to do that upon which we had agreed.

We knew exactly what we needed to do – whom we would incarnate as and when. We knew who would incarnate with us. Among them, we recognised those who would either hinder or help us to such an extent that the emotions and patterns of behaviour that had imprinted upon us in previous incarnations would be stimulated and ready for release. Exhilaration amplified our impatience, to the point where the soul who had honed the ability to sense balance whilst incarnate could stand it no more. It extended a thread of itself to the body of a developing female human and then oozed down the thread from its anchor in the oneness. As she settled into her new body, she affirmed to herself her determination to let me help her bring awareness of the truth of existence to the human race.

I Am. I am Am.

Her dam shivered as, all of a sudden, the name she would call her baby appeared in her mind. She had never heard it before, in fact she wasn't even sure it was a name. She shook her head determinedly and rubbed her swollen belly. She didn't care what anyone said. She knew her baby's name, and that was that. Senses Balance and I had chosen very well.

My attention turned to she who had agreed to be my dam. While she was already incarnate, she was as aware of me as she would have been if she were pure consciousness, for that is the way of the species she and I had chosen for so many of our incarnations. She acknowledged my attention before turning back to her earthly concerns of finding nutrition and fluid; she would nourish herself well before she encouraged the attention of her herd's breeding male, despite knowing that her next offspring would not contribute to her herd for long.

She knew that while I was practised at living as one of her kind, I would carry a difference that would be obvious to the rest; in a time when most of our kind lived apart from humans, I had agreed to be one of the few who would leave my herd in order to connect with and educate a human. Such agreements were accepted by my kind as necessary and, while not common, had occurred for generations. This agreement was different though. This time, I would not merely be helping my bonded human. I would bond to one who would be capable of helping me, and through me, all our kind. Those of us who bonded to humans had always carried the energetic signature of such an agreement, but I and a few others of my kind, who would be the instigators of a sudden and rapid evolution of our species, carried a much stronger one. We had already been named by the ancestors of a third species, who would evolve alongside us.

We were The Horses Of The New Dawn.

We would not follow the example of those who had gone before us. We would not compromise ourselves indefinitely in order to accommodate the learning and healing needs of our chosen human. We would insist that they recognise our now urgent need for balance, and we would demand that they do whatever they must in order to meet that need – for in the way of the world of the incarnate, in helping us, they could not help but help themselves.

Senses Balance and I had touched each of the other Horses Of The New Dawn during our revelling and preparation for our next incarnation, but now that she was busy settling into and shaping her new human body, I focused on them to the exclusion of all else.

They were all already incarnate, and most of them were already bonded to the humans whose souls they had identified during previous lives as possessing the experience and desire necessary for difficult, radical change. They were immediately aware of my attention and embraced it, following my lead into a whirling accumulation of joint purpose whose momentum gathered until we exploded into the smallest fragments of ourselves, only to redefine ourselves as a single entity an instant later.

The entity was an infinitely patient teacher whilst impatient to achieve its goal. It was almost entirely composed of energy of the heart, rendering the part of it that was not – the part that had suffered – burdensome to the extreme.

The Horses Of The New Dawn, as that single, powerful entity, could have released that which burdened it in an instant were it possible to do so with thought alone. But the injuries of its components had been amassed whilst incarnate, where the mechanism that drives the ebb and flow of existence is balance. Where balance had been disrupted, energy would remain trapped until it was restored.

The entity knew it and wouldn't allow us to remain as such for long. But while we were a part of it, we revelled in the strength of our joint purpose. We soared through the grey, welcoming the encouragement of all the souls we touched as we dipped and spun, picking up ever increasing momentum for our cause.

We whirled and swirled until our entity of joint purpose exploded into the constituent parts whose primary focus must now be the action upon which we had agreed in the physical world.

The other Horses funnelled most of themselves back down the thread connecting each of them to the body they were currently incarnating. The part of each that remained in the greyness with me began to push and prod gently at me, amplifying my sense of readiness to incarnate.

I allowed myself to be aware of all time and was immediately drawn to the instant when the growing foetus that would house me was ready for me to pervade her developing tissues. I poured myself down the thread of awareness that had found her at the perfect moment and intertwined myself with her genetics to influence who she would become.

Chapter Four

I can't do anything right. You'd think Mum and Dad would be happy I spend so much time in the library while my friends are playing games or getting up to mischief. You'd think they'd be proud of me for being such a fast reader now, and for having such neat handwriting for my age. All they want though, is for me to stop reading about the Horse-Bonded and filling more notebooks with my research, and for me to "stop obsessing about horses, especially the one you keep going on about who probably doesn't even exist". She does exist though. She must do, I've seen her in my mind. And I'm not going to stop learning everything I can about horses. I want to be sure that when she tugs me, I'll know how to care for her. So there.

Diary of Amarilla Nixon, aged 11

HER DAM WAS FINELY BONED and graceful in both body and spirit. Her sire was taller and a little heavier in build, and had the strength and willpower to race the wind and win. Their developing filly had the potential to be the best of both of them until I became part of her. The aspects of my previous incarnations that burdened my soul infiltrated her body along with the rest of me, affording it imperfections in places where it had been pure. I was, however, able to improve it with the benefit of my experience in other places where it carried inherited weaknesses. As her body continued to develop, I explored it thoroughly and constantly, familiarising myself with it and shaping it further until it felt like a comfortable home for my developing mind.

I felt my sire's fortitude beating through my body with my life fluid. I felt my dam's suppleness of mind expressed in every developing tissue. I had chosen well the body that had become mine, and felt a fresh determination to release the burdens I would express through my physicality.

As my time to breathe air drew close, I focused much of my attention on my dam's movement. I allowed my awareness of her body to sit within my own, so that I would emerge knowing how to stand and co-ordinate my limbs as I stood up, turned, and increased and decreased speed. I drew her awareness of her environment into my being so that I would be able to make sense of my physical surroundings as soon as I entered them.

My dam sensed the touch of my mind on hers and approved of both my preparation and my keenness to survive. She perceived me as part of her and always would. But while she had been prepared for the difference that would distinguish me not only from her but from the herd and most our kind, she was surprised by its magnitude; by the intensity of purpose that fuelled my efforts to be as strong in body and mind as possible by the time she birthed me.

As such, she spent almost as much time focusing on my movements within her whilst I sought to make my body my own, as I did on hers whilst she meandered about selecting food, occasionally shaking her head and neck to encourage a herd member out of her way; led her family and friends with a purposeful stride when it was time to change location; and occasionally flew across the ground at top speed, her heart thundering deafeningly as she led them away from danger.

She also explored the mind that I had begun preparing in order that when the time came, it could meet the needs of Senses Balance in this new incarnation of ours. Where most of our kind moved through life via a combination of group perception, the instinct of our species and the voice of our soul, I would need to have a very definite sense of my own mind; I would need to perceive myself as far more of an individual than was normal for my kind if I were to be up to the task of educating my human, and demanding from her in equal measure. Once I was born, I would need to focus upon learning how to use my body and survive in an unfamiliar landscape, so I wanted my mind to be ready and waiting when the time came to give it more of my attention.

My dam understood, without giving the matter any thought but merely by responding to the intense energy pattern inside her, that I needed as much time as possible to continue my endeavour before the trials of life took me away from it. She rested more than she normally would while carrying a foal. She delayed leading the herd to new locations, and when she did, they were forced to match her less than energetic pace. She moved around more carefully, more precisely. She did everything she could to avoid stress to her body so that it would house me for as long as I needed it to.

Only when I finally allowed my body to signal to hers, along the cord that joined us, that I was ready, did she select a suitable spot and prepare for my birth. The strength of the herd immediately became ours. They did not approach my dam physically, but their energy flowed towards us, gently enclosing and suffusing us so that we had all the strength we needed, and more.

I sensed the echoes of my dam's previous labours. Where her first had been prolonged and involved much pacing, sweating and discomfort, those that had followed had become progressively easier. She now merely shifted in place each time her body contracted around mine, and waited for her body to follow the path it knew so well. My body responded to hers and shifted within her so that my forelimbs and head would be expelled first. When the fluid surrounding me suddenly disappeared, the pressure of her body against mine increased.

I would be born immediately. I had spent the necessary time shaping and preparing my body and mind to be ideal for the mission that awaited me, and since that phase of my existence was now at an end, I would enter the next without delay.

My dam sensed my determination and lay down so that all her strength could be diverted to my urgency. As she pushed harder, she drew on the herd's energy, combining it with her own. She soon ejected my forelimbs and head, and the rest of my body followed with her next push, so that I landed on the ground behind her.

As I gasped my first painful breath in this life, my mind flew to my soul's memory of the final breath it had taken in its last… and from there, to Senses Balance. Except that wasn't who she was this time around. Her ability to sense balance and its antithesis remained intact, but was over-ridden by the single-mindedness and strength of character we had agreed she would need in order to succeed where previously she had faltered.

Walks A Straight Path. That was who she was. She was in her twelfth summer, and she was healthy in body and sound of mind. I felt her hesitate in her task as she sensed my attention, and quickly pulled away from her. Satisfied that we were both present and intact, I focused on my side of our agreement. I would ensure I survived to be her Bond-Partner.

I felt a momentary sense of loss and panic as the cord broke that had connected me to my dam for my entire physical existence so far. Her warm breath soothed me even as her tongue worked its way around my body, reassuring me that she had not abandoned me – that she would take as good care of me now that my body was outside hers as she had when it had been safely protected inside.

I explored the feeling of air entering and leaving my body, fascinated by the sudden increase in my craving for it as the shock of my first breaths subsided. Once breathing felt like a natural thing to do, I felt an urgency to support myself on my limbs – to move, to gain control of my body. Every moment of delay increased the chance I would not survive, and survive I must.

My preparation served me well, and I made it to my feet on my first attempt. Echoes of my previous body's strength and co-ordination taunted me, even as they combined with my memory of my dam's movement to show me how to move my limbs, so that I remained upright as I wobbled from one foot to the next.

My dam lay back down on the ground as her body prepared to expel the last part of her physical connection to me. I wobbled around her prone, contracting body, keen to improve my command of my legs so that I didn't feel so vulnerable.

By the time my dam returned to her feet, a feeling was stealing over me, one that was foreign to my young body yet familiar to the echoes of my past. My experienced dam knew exactly what I needed and positioned herself so that her belly and hind limb were by my nose. I reached out tentatively, and as soon as I touched her leg, instinct drove me to suck on it. She shifted so that I lost my grip and attached to her belly instead. She shifted again, and I found what I needed. I sensed her elation and contentment amplifying mine as I took in the goodness her body was so keen to provide mine. I felt stronger and more a part of the world into which she had propelled me. I felt safe and nurtured and protected… and, all of a sudden, as if I had done all I could for now.

My body knew to fold its forelimbs in order to lie down, and as I returned to the ground for the first time in this incarnation, my ears flickered at the memory of the loud bangs that had accompanied my previous body's somersault to its final resting place. The memory faded as my dam breathed the energy of her heart into mine, and my body and mind sank into a deep, restful sleep.

Chapter Five

Now I know for definite that she exists. I didn't just see her in my mind, I felt her – not within my mind as such, but more like a whisper that passed me by. I'm so excited, but I can't tell anyone as they'll just say it was wishful thinking. It wasn't. It was definitely her. Something has changed, it's like she's closer, somehow. She'll tug me one day, I know it.

Diary of Amarilla Nixon, aged 11¼

I WOKE to a cacophony of sounds, funnelled by my well developed ears to my inexperienced brain. I staggered to my feet, my heart beating my life fluid around my body with such force, it felt as if it might burst out of me in a multitude of places. I tried to grasp what was happening and what I should do, but I couldn't; there was so much noise, so much movement, I was overwhelmed.

My dam flashed in front of me, shrieking and showing her teeth to one of our herd. I sensed his surprise and fear as he spun away from her and ran back to his dam. My own dam had always been kind and gentle to him, often watching over him while his dam rested, so he had been unprepared for her hostility. His dam kept her distance, and I sensed her understanding of the situation even as my dam shrieked again and ran at full speed towards the member of our herd who now stood closest to me. When she too fled to the distance that the rest of the herd appeared to have judged safe, my dam stood, her sides heaving, staring from one to another of them. They all lifted and lowered their heads as they looked between her and me, sniffing the air and registering the scent of their herd's newest member.

Sniffing was acceptable to my dam. Approaching any closer was not. They knew that now. However close a relationship they had enjoyed with her before I was born, none of them were now more important to her than I. While I was so small and vulnerable, she would allow no one near me – not even those she trusted to watch over her while she slept – and since she was so highly respected within the herd, she would not need to tell them again.

I felt as safe and as nurtured as I had whilst within her belly. I sidled over to her, wary in case she might launch herself into another attack if any of the herd moved a foot the wrong way by mistake. She made a low, comforting sound that reassured me I was as welcome to approach her as the rest of the herd were not. The energy of her heart enfolded me and drew me to her until I was once more in position to take the goodness of her body into mine.

By the time my belly was full, the rest of the herd had wandered away. Many had their heads down and were pulling at nutrition that was erupting out of the ground. Some were lying down, and a few were running and jumping around. Their excitement and enjoyment lifted the energy of the rest of the herd, including my dam. Having rested whilst I slept, she was keen to recall how her body could move without my weight and bulk. She jumped away from me with her forelimbs and then moved all four of her limbs so that two were in the air while two were on the ground. Immediately, I felt an urge to follow her. I was jubilant when my legs followed my intention for them to move in the same arrangement as hers, and gratified that it felt natural and comfortable to move that way after all my preparation whilst in her body. I sensed my dam's satisfaction that I was able to keep up with her, albeit within a small area, and her keenness to reinforce my instinct to follow her whenever she moved away from me.

We changed direction and speed a few times, but then my limbs felt less easy to move. My dam was instantly aware of my predicament and came to a stop. It was only when her feet and mine ceased pounding on the ground, and my heart stopped its wild thumping in my chest, that I registered a new sound. My dam moved slowly enough towards it that I could follow her. When we saw something moving ahead of us, she stopped. I sensed her anticipation and realised it was comparable to my own when I wanted the fluid goodness that her body provided mine. I absorbed her experience of our surroundings and knew from the fluid's scent that it was clean and fresh. She took me closer until splashes of it leapt into the air just before us, but then, despite her craving for it, moved no further until I gave in to my body's weariness and lay down. She remained at my side until I was too sleepy to rise, then approached the fluid. It cooled and revitalised her as she drew it into her body. Her relief and satisfaction soothed me to sleep.

I focused, throughout the light and dark spells that followed, on fulfilling my body's requirements. I suckled and slept whenever I needed to, safe in the knowledge that my dam would protect me.

When I was on my feet and she moved off, I was sure to explore my rapidly increasing repertoire of movements whilst following her. I leapt and spun, and when I landed, I threw my hind limbs out behind me, enjoying the feel of their increasing strength and co-ordination. Then I stood on them and waved my forelimbs in the air, proud to feel heat reaching my belly from its provider in the expanse above.

I enjoyed the admiring stares of the rest of my herd, and my dam's pride and satisfaction, for they were warranted; I had a good command of my body for one so young, a mind that processed information rapidly, and a determined soul that blazed with anticipation for the life ahead of me. When the herd was ready to move on – at a time that I knew would be determined by my dam – I would not hinder them, and whilst I remained one of their number, I would be valuable to them.

I was delighted when my dam joined me in my wild explorations of what my body could do, and revelled in mirroring her movements as she danced across the ground with me. She only broke from our game in order to remind other youngsters, who were keen to join in, to keep their distance from me.

I experienced the exchange of light with darkness many times before my dam began taking me closer to other dams with youngsters at their tails. She would warn any not of her choosing out of the space she had decided we would occupy, and they obeyed her without a hint of defiance.

Though I initially felt a little wary at being near others whose bodies were so much larger than mine, the delight radiating from the youngsters combined with the heart energy flowing from my dam to dispel my concern. When my dam dropped her head to the ground to gather nutrition, I leapt around by her side, showing off my body. My heart beat harder when a young female sped past me, flicking her feet out in front of her, inviting me to copy her.

Resolve slowed and softened my heart; copy her I would. I would learn from each and every one of my kind who had something to teach me, so that when the time came to leave the herd, I would take the best of each of them with me; I would be the best I could possibly be.

I took that resolve with me when my dam finally allowed me to interact with members of the herd other than tolerant dams and their fragile young. Instinct ensured that I clacked my teeth together when I approached those much older and stronger than I, so that I reminded them of my youth, vulnerability and lack of intention to advance my social position. Instinct had them believing me even when I showed boldness by inviting them to play with me in order that I could continue to strengthen and learn.

By the time I no longer needed my dam's body to sustain mine, I could move the other youngsters out of my way with a stare, regardless of how much older and larger they were. By the time I reached my second summer, most of the herd – my dam and sire being notable exceptions – would respect my presence and be ready to move, play or engage in mutual, pleasurable biting at my request. I had learnt every lesson I could incite them to teach me, and consistently expressed my understanding of how to be one of our kind with a strength of will that discouraged argument.

For the first time since I was born, I turned my attention away from purely surviving and learning, to the reason for it all; Walks A Straight Path, the soul for whom my own yearned. I was relieved to sense that she was healthy, and I was gratified but not at all surprised to find that she had been as dedicated as I to learning anything that would serve us both. She was tired from using her mind to identify herbs that could heal us… but not too tired to sense the touch of my mind on hers.

I recoiled from her, knowing it was too early for her to sense my location and come looking for me. When the time came for us to meet, the strength of our bond would combine with the echoes of our past to ensure that we proceeded at pace along the path we had agreed to tread, and neither of us were ready for that yet; we needed to be stronger and more mature.

But her soul's yearning was equal to mine, as was her determination. She probed after me, intent on finding the mind whose touch she had recognised. It took all my concentration to remain out of her reach, to the extent that by the time she finally gave up, my body was sore in a multitude of places due to biters having taken advantage of my preoccupation.

As soon as I ceased actively avoiding her, she was back, probing along the thread of attention I had extended to her in my curiosity. I stamped at the biters swarming around my limbs and swiped at those attempting to land on my belly. If I were to avoid my body going into a fierce defence response as a result of more bites, I would need to retain a level of focus on my surroundings.

I extended a little of myself along the thread to Walks A Straight Path and sensed her pause her probing of the sensation of my nearness. When she resumed her probing towards me, trying to touch the mind she could sense just beyond hers, I pulled back, further beyond her reach. She learnt quickly and pulled back in turn. I extended myself towards her again and was delighted by her joy at my nearness; I knew she would take comfort from it whilst respecting the boundary I had established. She tempered her passion with intelligence, and she trusted the voice of her soul as well as her instincts. She was the human for whom my kind had waited so long, and she was everything we had hoped she would be.

Chapter Six

I learnt about the Woeful today. I don't think I've ever felt so scared as when Nerys told me they hunt horses. I feel sorry for the Woeful, I do, but my horse is out there, and the thought of anything happening to her absolutely terrifies me. She doesn't seem bothered by her vulnerability though. I can see her in my mind, lying in the leaves alongside her herd and feeling just about as serene as it's possible to be.

Diary of Amarilla Nixon, aged 14½

AS WE MATURED, I would frequently sense Walks A Straight Path extending herself along the thread to where I ensured a part of my mind constantly resided. She always stopped short of the boundary I had established, but her mind's proximity to mine allowed her to sense aspects of my life that previously she had been forced to conjure up in her imagination. She always experienced joy at sensing the current object of my focus, my surroundings and my state of mind. When she was enduring the challenges that were shaping her, she absorbed the peace of my herd as if she were a part of it, which in truth she was, even if her human mind wasn't yet capable of knowing it.

Whilst I knew that the distance between us was necessary, I found it difficult at times to remain steadfast about preventing Walks A Straight Path from immersing herself in our bond; her mind was as perfect a fit for mine as our souls had intended, and I had no doubt that our bodies would complement one another equally well, just as we had envisaged. But steadfast I remained. I would not fail her by enabling her to come to me before time.

I learnt all I could from the horses of my herd, and when there was nothing more to learn, I turned my attention towards those who shared my purpose. I would learn from the other Horses Of The New Dawn.

They all acknowledged my focus upon them instantly, and, in the way of our kind, were immediately aware of everything that had occurred in my life so far, including my contact with Walks A Straight Path. Some of them extended the energy of their heart to their human partner as a reflex, reinforcing the bond that had held firm between them from their previous incarnation together, to this.

There would be useful details I could learn from them, and I would explore their experiences with their partner until I found them. I was drawn first to the experiences of the male who was now known as Gas.

Gas had not incarnated many times previously. When he had, he always chose to be one of our kind, and most of those times, including in his previous incarnation, he chose a life living in a herd that roamed the plains, avoiding all who were not our kind – until, in his previous incarnation, he couldn't.

He had been a gentle, unassuming member of his herd, and as such, he had been allowed to remain a part of it for longer than the stallion usually tolerated. He had begun to sense, however, that his presence near the breeding females would not be borne much longer, and so was unsurprised when the stallion – who was also his sire – came at him shortly after the provider of light chased away the darkness. His dam called to him, but rather than the call to come close she had used while raising him, it was a quieter, resigned call of farewell.

He didn't resist. He ran from the stallion as fast as his limbs would allow and didn't look back, or even pause, until long after the stallion had ceased his chase. He sensed where a herd of displaced young males like himself were roaming together, providing one another with company, safety and the opportunity to practise behaviour they had witnessed in older stallions, so that one day they might win their own herd. He would go to them and run with them until he felt stronger.

He headed in their direction at a steady speed, keen to reach them as soon as possible in order to relieve the vulnerability he was feeling at being alone and unprotected for the first time in his young life. He was experienced enough, however, to know that when his body clamoured for sustenance, he should comply with its demands. His coat was wet due to his body's efforts to rid itself of the heat of the season, and his feet throbbed as a result of sustained pounding on the dry, cracked ground. He would welcome a spell of standing in cool fluid while drawing it into his body. As soon as he scented some, he diverted towards it. He slowed his pace so that he could divert a greater amount of his attention to exploring his awareness of the area; while he was at rest, bathing and drinking, he would be even more vulnerable to predators than he was at present.

He missed his dam intensely all of a sudden. She was aware of him, but for the first time since he was born, she did not extend the energy of her heart to him, for it would not help him. If he were to survive independently of her, he must not yearn for her, but should instead focus all his attention on his surroundings and his body's needs. She even pushed at him slightly. Her reminder had the desired effect, and he brought his attention fully back to the ground in front of him and his awareness of everything that breathed in his immediate vicinity and beyond.

He had done everything his dam and herd had taught him. He should have been safe, but he had no way of knowing that the ground would suddenly disappear from under his feet. One moment, he was almost upon the pool he had been seeking to cool his body and relieve his thirst, and the next, all he could see around him was brown earth. Panicked, he tried to jump up towards the heat provider, but he had no room either to bend his hind limbs or lift his forelimbs. He thrashed from side to side, but all he achieved was to bring down a cloud of dry earth on top of himself. He screamed even though it went against all his instincts to make a noise that would attract predators; his terror at being trapped was greater. He screamed again and thrashed about with his limbs and torso, then stopped to expel from his throat the shower of earth that again descended upon him.

He stopped screaming, but continued to flail and squirm until exhaustion prevented it. His limbs buckled beneath him, yet he was held above them by the earth that refused him his freedom.

The heat provider was low in the sky when his ears flickered at a distant sound. His awareness warned him that predators were approaching – a large group of them. Panic gave him a fresh burst of strength, and he fought again to create any amount of space that would allow him to jump clear of his prison.

The noise made by the predators increased, and he sensed them approaching at greater speed as they sighted the fluid that all who breathed needed to survive. When their scent reached him, it confirmed that which he already knew, both from his experience of them in previous incarnations and from the collective consciousness of our kind; these were the worst kind of predators, for they alone pretended to be otherwise. Many of them even convinced themselves that they were benign, only revealing their true nature when faced with challenge. The approaching predators were human.

He stilled his body. He could scent no bloodlust upon them, so they weren't actively hunting. Humans couldn't hear or scent as well as other predators and had no awareness beyond their physical senses, so maybe if he drew no attention to himself, they would pass him by without even noticing he was there.

'Hello, what have we here?' a voice said. A clod of earth landed on the captive's back, causing him to renew his effort to thrash around and free himself.

'Looks like dinner to me,' another said. 'Look at it, all stuck down an 'ole, waiting for me to load ma' gun and blow its brains out.'

'What the hell, Collins, stop!' a weaker, more hesitant voice said.

'Well, look who's found his voice. About bleedin' time,' the second voice sneered. 'Did you find it when you were told to interrogate those deserters we found a way back? No, siree, you did not. Did you even find it when you were told to tell Wilson to interrogate them? Still a big fat no. But now, when there's – what is that, an 'orse? – when there's an 'orse all trussed up and ready for us to feast on 'im, now you remember you can speak.'

Chapter Six

The weaker voice sounded stronger this time. 'I've followed all orders that don't involve torturing anyone, and I'm not going to let you shoot that horse.'

'What is that, a sinkhole?' another voice interrupted. 'Must have taken his feet out from under him. Not surprising in this drought, the water level underground has dropped that much, it's leaving weaknesses. We ought to be more careful where we're putting our feet from now on.'

'Before we go anywhere, we have to dig the horse out of there,' the rapidly strengthening voice said.

The laughter of many human males terrified the captive at their feet even further; the sound wasn't just loud, it was menacing.

'We'll shoot him, cut him up and then hand out pieces of him, that's what we'll do,' the first voice said.

'Over my dead body. He's a horse, not a deserter or even an enemy soldier. We have food with us, so we don't need to eat him. We need to free him.' The human who was now blazing with purpose for the first time in his life threw himself across the hole.

The captive stilled beneath him, drawing his breath in and blowing it out hard and fast, convinced his time to leave his incarnation must have come, even as the voice of his soul told him otherwise. His breathing began to ease as he allowed himself to believe his sense that the predator now closest to him was protecting him, shielding him with his human body as his dam had done so many times when he was small. He sensed the kinship the human felt with him; he knew how it felt to be trapped, helpless to change his circumstances. He also sensed the human's terror of meeting the end of his existence, something he had gone to extremes to avoid... until now.

'Why, you jumped up...'

'Can it, Mac, remember who his pa is,' a new voice said.

'I don't care who sired this pathetic excuse for a soldier, he's under my command and he'll do as I bloody well tell him. Get out of the way, Theroux, I'm having horse for dinner.'

'I'm sorry, I know this is going to scare you even more, but it's the only way,' Theroux whispered to the captive before lowering himself onto his earth-covered back and arranging himself along it. 'If you shoot him, your bullet will have to pass through me,' he said loudly.

'I'm ordering you to remove yourself from that hole,' Mac said, his voice hard with rage and promised violence.

'What's going on here?' a loud, sharp voice said. 'Sergeant MacCartney, explain.'

The captive sensed the humans rearranging themselves so that they stood taller but with an air of meekness.

'Theroux is not only disobeying a direct order, Sir, he's arguing with me like I ain't got stripes on my arm. There's a horse down there that's fallen down a sinkhole. It'll feed all of us this evening, but he's intent on digging it out and freeing it.'

There was a pause. Then the sharp voice said, 'MacCartney, you will order your men to watch every step they take on their way to the waterhole, so they don't join the horse. As soon as they've had a drink and refilled their canteens, we'll be on our way.' When his order had been carried out by all but Theroux, he continued talking to Mac in a quiet voice. 'If Theroux wants to remain behind and dig the horse out, let him; he'll be doing us a favour. We have witnesses he defied orders, and while his father's status prevents us from shooting him as a deserter, it doesn't prevent us from leading our men to food and shelter while he kills himself trying to free a godforsaken horse. If he doesn't die of heat exhaustion, and whatever made those tracks we passed a while back doesn't kill him, the horse will when it gets out; it's clearly as wild as they come.'

Chapter Six

'But, Cap'n Davis...'

'That's an order, MacCartney. Join your men and be ready to head out in twenty.' When Mac's footsteps had faded away, the voice, no less sharp for its low tone, said, 'Did you hear that, Theroux? You've got your own way, just like always. We're leaving you to do as you will with the horse. Dig it out, talk to it, sleep beside it and read it fairy tales, it's no odds to me; you'll be dead before tomorrow's out, and your father will probably thank me. You've been an embarrassment to him since the day you were born – flunking school, failing officer training when you were only accepted because of his name, then barely competent enough even to join us on campaign as a foot soldier – between you and me, I don't think he's your father; a man of his calibre could never have sired an insubordinate weakling like you.'

Theroux didn't utter a word in response to the male who goaded him, instead whispering a constant stream of reassurances to the panicked captive beneath him. 'I'm so sorry, I know I'm scaring you, but I'm not going to hurt you. If I get off you before they leave, they'll shoot you to spite me, so I have to stay here to protect you. As soon as they leave, I'll get you water and something to eat, then I'll set about digging you out of there. I won't hurt you. I'll protect you. I won't hurt you. I'll protect you. I won't hurt you. I'll protect you...'

He was so intent on trying to calm the captive, he didn't notice the sharp voiced human leaving to join the others, or even the group as a whole moving off in a line of barely contained violence and misery. It was only when the captive stopped trembling beneath him that Theroux noticed there was silence where there had been shouting and raucous laughter. 'There, they've gone,' he said, his voice low and soft. 'Thank the Lord. It's just you and me now.'

Theroux looked about himself, trying to decide how best to

climb off the exhausted captive beneath him without causing more distress. He could easily reach the edge of the hole if he sat up, and if he stood, he could step out. Standing might cause discomfort or even pain though, and he thought the captive was beginning to trust him.

'I'm going to sit up very slowly,' he said, his voice soft and even, 'and then I'm going to put a leg over your neck, which you're going to find very scary. Then, I'm going to use the grass to pull myself out. I'm sorry, I'll be as quick as I can.' He stroked the length of the captive's neck with long, slow movements. 'I won't hurt you, trust me, I'm here to protect you. I won't hurt you, trust me, I'm here to protect you...'

Theroux repeated the words over and over, and despite the captive not recognising the sound of them, he felt them. And he believed them. Having a predator on his back was the worst possible challenge to his survival that he could face, but this human did not behave like a predator. While his sounds, movements and behaviour were unfamiliar, he swaddled the captive with the energy of his heart without even knowing he was doing such, and the universal language did not lie. The captive accepted Theroux's energy and gave him his trust. He did not tremble or thrash when the human shifted upon his back, or even when his weight disappeared, causing a fresh shower of crumbling earth to land on the captive in its place.

'There we are, well done, my friend. Now, I'm going to fill up my canteen from the waterhole, then I'll be right back. I think you can drink from my bowl, can't you? It'll take a while for you to drink your fill that way, but since I don't have a bucket, it'll have to do. To be honest, I'm surprised they left me my pack – I suppose it's because my name's on everything; they'd have a hard time explaining how they had my stuff if they were meant to have left me alive. Listen to me, chatting away to you like you understand me… yet funnily enough, I felt like you did understand me just then, like you might even trust me a little. Fancy that, eh! I finally find someone willing to believe in me, and it's a horse.' He turned and walked away, still talking. 'So, then, I'd better hurry up and do what I said I would, so you know your trust is warranted. Hang in there, fella, I'll be right back.'

Chapter Seven

FAO: Lieutenant-General Keele
FROM: Captain Davis
SUBJECT: Private Theroux
Please inform General Theroux of a most regrettable incident regarding his son. Having already disobeyed two direct orders, Private Theroux refused to stand aside whilst his sergeant shot a trapped wild horse, then he deserted his regiment in order to free it. He is now missing, presumed dead.

THE HEAT PROVIDER had dropped out of sight by the time Theroux had fetched enough fluid – "water", he called it – that the captive would take no more. In what light there still was, he pulled nutrition – "grass" – from the edges of the waterhole and then held it out for the captive to take from him.

When the captive began to shift about, Theroux said, 'You're feeling stronger and now you're even more desperate to get out. I get it. Just let me have something to eat and drink, then I'll set about digging you out.' He showed his teeth, and I sensed his heart feeling lighter as he freed an implement that had been attached to his bundle of possessions. 'Happily for us, I have a shovel. I wonder who they'll make dig the latrine holes now, and what they'll make him dig it with.'

He sat down by the captive and continued to try to keep him calm using his voice; he had no idea that it was the energy of his heart that was having more of an effect.

The heat and light provider was in no position to offer either by the time Theroux finished eating, got to his feet and picked up his shovel. He looked upward. 'Luck is on our side again, my friend. The moon is full, there isn't a cloud in the sky, and there's no one around to insist on lighting a fire and killing my night vision. Now, where to start? I think probably here, a little way in front of you, and I'll work my way down towards you at an angle. That way you can get used to me throwing soil around from a distance to begin with, before I dig a ramp down towards your front legs. I just hope there aren't any rocks in the way.'

He lifted the shovel and slammed it into the ground. 'And hopefully… I… won't… end… up… in… a… hole… myself.' He spoke each word in between impaling the ground and throwing mounds of it to one side. 'Nope… the… ground… seems… firm. Rock… hard… actually. You… were… just… unlucky… to… find… the…exact… spot… where… the… earth… had… become… unstable.' He stopped talking as his breath came faster and sharper.

He ceased moving the earth from time to time in order to turn and slowly survey his surroundings. He knew that the waterhole that had attracted him and the captive would attract others, and was resolute in his intention to protect both of them from any threat. He repeatedly picked up an instrument and held it up high so he could look along its length, turning a full circle as he checked for predators.

Had he been as aware of the captive as the captive was of him, he would have taken heart from knowing that the only active breathers in the vicinity were small hoppers and hissing sliders, both of which avoided those larger than themselves. The captive knew that should he sense the approach of a predator, he would need to make his discomfort known to Theroux in a physically obvious way, but he was confident that if it came to that, the human would understand and protect him.

He was behaving so unlike most humans who had contributed to the collective experience of our kind. He had been willing to single himself out from his herd despite being the weakest of them physically, when all know that is the quickest way to attract the attention of predators of all kinds. He did the bidding of the voice of his soul despite not being consciously aware of it. And he radiated the energy of his heart despite not having had a parent capable of showing him how.

His behaviour was even more remarkable for the fact that until then, he had allowed his life to be ruled by an uncommonly potent fear of death. Like most humans, he believed that when his body expired, so would he, but unlike most of them, he didn't put that knowledge to one side so that he might enjoy his life. He held it up in front of himself almost constantly… until he had been ordered to inflict suffering on others of his kind, and then again when he felt a sudden, overwhelming urge to protect the captive from harm. His fear of ceasing to exist was a constant undercurrent to his thoughts and outlook, yet had been overpowered by the energy of his heart when others were in danger of suffering or coming to an end themselves. It seemed that whilst radiating the energy of his heart to those who needed it, he was receptive to the voice of his soul guiding him towards balance.

The captive, like all of our kind, was a bringer of balance. Being trapped in a hole in Theroux's path through life was exactly where he needed to be. He was aware of his protector's exhaustion, yet Theroux continued to move the earth through the entirety of the darkness. His weakness and weariness forced him to take longer and longer breaks, but at no time would he sit down, for he feared his body would succumb to sleep. He had promised that he would protect and free the captive, and he would not betray the trust the captive was affording him.

The light provider had just appeared at the opposite end of the expanse from where it had disappeared, when Theroux threw down his shovel. There was now only a slim wall of earth between him and the captive who stood watching him, his eyes mirroring the exhaustion of his protector. Theroux tentatively reached out a forelimb towards the captive, who immediately lifted his head as high as he could, his eyes wide. Theroux ceased his forelimb's advancement but did not withdraw it. The captive slowly lowered his head and stretched it towards Theroux. He sniffed the offered forelimb, despite already being familiar with the human's scent. Then he touched it with the sensitive part of his nose, breathing deeply and slowly, communicating his acceptance of the human's proximity.

'I need you to understand what I'm going to tell you,' Theroux told him, 'and for no reason that I can justify, I think you will. I think you're too tired to kick through this last lot of soil before making it up the ramp, so I'm going to dig it out of your way. I need you to stay where you are until I've done that and then made it up the ramp before you. Please be patient, as I'm tired and won't be able to get up there very quickly. If you try to get out while I'm still on the ramp, you'll crush me. I'm trusting you as you've trusted me, alright?' He drew in a deep breath and blew it back out. 'Right, then, let's do this.'

As he forced his shovel into the wall, his fear of death reared up in front of him like a stallion defending his young, and he almost threw down his implement and fled. The captive lifted his head suddenly at the change in atmosphere, his eyes showing white where there would normally only have been brown, and his body trembling.

Theroux's own eyes widened at the sight of his fear being manifested in another. He couldn't bear it and was immediately consumed by the energy of his heart at the sight of the captive's distress. The captive relaxed and amplified Theroux's energy with that from his own heart, so that the human could not help but feel it and know that fear had no place between them.

'I trust you,' Theroux said. And this time, he meant it.

He lifted the earth and, with tired forelimbs, threw it up high out of the hole, without once looking at the captive to check he was standing in place. When no more earth stood between the two of them, he leant back against the wall of earth behind him until his breathing was deeper and slower, before nodding to the captive and then turning his back to him and walking slowly, painfully up the ramp.

The instant he was out of sight, the captive burst out of the hole behind him, his desperation to be free fuelling his body to do that which should have been impossible after his ordeal. When he reached the top, his instinct was to keep going until he reached the waterhole, but the energy of his heart halted him in place on limbs that shook with weariness and lack of nourishment; the human had succumbed to his body's exhaustion and lay unconscious next to the implement that had taken the skin from his hands and the strength from his body whilst he used it to free the captive.

Captive-no-longer nudged him with his nose. The human

didn't respond. Captive-no-longer looked longingly at the glistening water a short distance away. It tantalised him with its fresh scent, as did the sweet scent of the grass surrounding it. The human needed to drink too. He should accompany Captive-no-longer to the water. He nudged the human again, but he had sunk too far into his slumber to be aware of anything.

Captive-no-longer raised his head and observed his surroundings in all directions whilst extending his awareness even further. There were no predators nearby. He and the human were safe for now. He would nourish his body while the human slept.

Chapter Eight

FAO: Captain Davis
SENDER: Lieutenant-General Keele
Subject: Private Theroux
The general has been informed of his son's fate. He has ordered that the circumstances be deemed confidential, and that any person disclosing them will be court-marshalled. While the general does not hold you accountable for his son's choices, he will hold you accountable if his order of confidentiality is disobeyed, and you will be court-marshalled alongside any offenders.

WATER HAD NEVER SEEMED SO sharp and grass never so sweet as that which Captive-no-longer took into his body following his return above ground. He drew in as much water as he could bear and snatched rapidly at the stalks of grass, knowing that the light provider's return would likely bring others to the waterhole. His instinct nagged constantly at him to reach the

Chapter Eight

safety of the herd he would join, but he needed to recover his strength if he were to comply with it. He also needed a period of slumber of the depth in which the human was engaging, but he would need to be far from the dangers of the waterhole, and in the company of those who would watch over him, before he could indulge in that. He would satisfy his thirst and hunger, rouse the human from his slumber and then be on his way to find his herd.

He knew that was the course of action he should take; the instinct of our kind repeatedly told him so. Yet the voice of his soul told him differently. It was gentler in its urging than his instinct. It did not demand he pay attention, yet when he did, he felt his connection to All That Is with greater intensity. While his instinct would have him acting out of fear in order to ensure his body's survival, his soul would have him remembering that in truth, he was always at peace; that when the energy of his heart fuelled his decisions, he would fulfil his role as a bringer of balance.

And so it was that when he sensed an approaching hunter, he did not run towards the herd that promised a measure of security, but to the human who had protected him and whom he would protect in return. When he nudged the human this time, it was with insistence. Theroux would wake and flee with him until they were beyond the hunter's senses. They would keep the waterhole between them and the hunter so that if she sensed or even came close even to scent them, it might provide a distraction and delay.

Theroux didn't move. His efforts to free Captive-no-longer had truly exhausted him, and his body resisted waking whilst it tried to repair itself. A flare of panic shot through Captive-no-longer as the hunter continued on her course towards them. Her awareness was blunted by her tendency to focus primarily upon scenting her prey, and since she was still some distance away and not directly downwind of them, she was as yet unaware of them, but that would not be the case for long.

Captive-no-longer's next nudge pushed Theroux from his front onto his back, and was accompanied by a scream that he couldn't risk discharging out loud. *Awaken! Danger approaches!*

While the human had but the barest sense of Captive-no-longer's emotions and desires when he was awake, his soul urged his mind to transform them into words whilst he was asleep.

Protector! Awaken! Danger!

The words prodded at the survival instinct rooted deep within Theroux's body, and he flung out a forelimb. 'Wha'? Wha's up?'

Captive-no-longer nudged him again, this time onto his side. *Awaken! A hunter approaches! We must flee!*

Theroux rolled onto his front, then drew his hind limbs underneath him and sat on them. 'A hunter's coming?' He looked about himself. 'How did I know that?' His eyes widened at the sight of Captive-no-longer standing over him.

We must flee. Now.

Theroux rubbed his eyes. 'I need water. I'm hallucinating. Do you know,' he said, looking up at Captive-no-longer, 'I could have sworn I just heard you talking to me in my head, yet common sense tells me you're not even there. You're a wild horse, you'll have been gone from here…' He paused to look up at the heat provider and then continued, 'You'll have been gone from here hours ago.'

He put his forelimbs to the ground and pushed himself backward onto his feet, on which he stood unsteadily. He instinctively reached out a forelimb to Captive-no-longer in order to stabilise himself. He gasped at the solid warmth that didn't balk from him. 'You're really here! Wait, did you watch over me while I slept? Huh?' He rubbed Captive-no-longer's shoulder. 'I know horses do that for each other, but I'm not a horse.' His words blended into one another as if he couldn't spare the effort to keep them separate.

You are a human who defied your fear in order to help me, Captive-no-longer informed him. *I defy my fear in order to help you in return. A hunter approaches. When she senses us, she will increase her speed. When she scents us, she will pursue us. We must leave before either happens.*

Captive-no-longer shifted on his feet and uttered a low, urgent sound in order to emphasise his point.

Theroux shook his head. 'While I don't believe I can really have heard what I think I just did, I'll get my gun.'

He took a step away from Captive-no-longer and immediately fell to the ground. He reached out and grasped the implement that he believed would protect them from predators, and began examining it. 'If there's something coming that wants us for breakfast, this should convince them otherwise. Wait. It's not loaded.' He fumbled around in his belongings until a sense of unease turned into intense, heart-thumping fear. 'They've taken my ammo. Bastards!'

Captive-no-longer uttered his low, urgent sound again and began to move at speed around Theroux, the human's fear amplifying his own to the extent that it almost drowned out the influence of his soul.

At the sight of him, Theroux was flooded with concern for the captive he had worked so hard to free, rendering him susceptible to the urging of his own soul. *I trust you.* He formed his thought using the energy of his heart and, as such, it reached Captive-no-longer through his fear. *If you tell me there's a hunter approaching, then I believe you. We should leave.*

Theroux used his gun to support himself while he once more got to his feet. He tried to pick up his belongings, but could no more lift them than he could walk when he attempted it. He looked up at Captive-no-longer, fear now pulsing through him with a ferocity that would soon have it descending into outright terror. *Death is coming for me. I have no escape, but you do. Go. I'll be easy prey for the hunter, and you'll be alive and free.* His fear stilled at the thought, his wish for Captive-no-longer to survive flowing out of him with the energy of his heart so that it was soft and nurturing, rather than harsh and commanding. *Go.*

Captive-no-longer ceased shifting his feet. *That is not balance. You helped me and I will help you.* His soul urged him to go further, and, immersed in the combined energy of his and Theroux's hearts, he did. *In so doing the connection between us will settle more firmly into place. Our bond will hold us together from this life into the next when we will elicit much change.* Captive-no-longer lowered himself to the ground beside Theroux. *You must sit on my back as you did when I was trapped. As you have upon others of my kind.*

Our WHAT will do WHAT?

HURRY. Captive-no-longer propelled his urging into Theroux's being with such force that the human's mind, so new to being conscious of its sensitivity, could offer no resistance. He gathered the little strength he had left and hauled himself onto Captive-no-longer's back, leaving all his belongings behind.

Where before, the horse's fear and captivity had rendered him weak and trembling beneath Theroux, now his bond with the human, and his awareness of the use to which they would put it, rendered him stronger than he had ever felt in his life. His elation transferred to Theroux and gave him the strength to clamp his limbs around Captive-no-longer as he got to his feet.

We are one. My strength is yours, Captive-no-longer told his human, and took flight.

Through Theroux, Captive-no-longer was aware of all the mounts the human had ridden before him, and drew on their experience until carrying a rider felt like a more natural thing to do. But where his mind was willing to carry his rider indefinitely to safety, his young and inexperienced body soon tired.

Theroux was immediately aware of it. *Stop. Please, stop and let me get down. You can't carry me any longer without causing harm to yourself. You took us away at such great speed that we must be beyond the senses of whatever was approaching the waterhole by now.*

Where Captive-no-longer had felt stronger than ever before, he now felt more tired than he could remember. Tired but fulfilled; Theroux had been aware of his mount's tiredness before he had recognised from experience the feel of a tired horse beneath him – he had felt Captive-no-longer's body as if it were his own. When Captive-no-longer had told him they were one, he had more than believed it; he had taken it into himself along with his mount's strength.

The two of them had done all that they needed to in this incarnation; they had established and cemented the bond that would take them closer to balance, and both of their species with them.

Captive-no-longer slowed his limbs, using all the experience he could sense through Theroux to keep them co-ordinated enough that his deceleration was smooth enough to not dislodge his rider. He had exhausted the young body that his protector had risked his life to save, to the point that neither of them now had a chance of surviving. They were alone on drought-ridden plains with no water or even shelter from the relentless heat provider. In escaping the hunter who would have feasted upon Theroux's body, they would now succumb to the landscape that would feast upon them both.

Theroux made it only a few steps after relieving his mount of his weight, before falling to the ground, his body lacking the strength to continue. Captive-no-longer's shaking limbs gave way, and he collapsed to the ground beside the human.

I did this to you, I'm so sorry, the human told his Bond-Partner, desperately trying – and failing – to swallow down his fear of ceasing to exist, lest it affect Captive-no-longer.

You did nothing but identify yourself as a soul who would partner mine to a greater purpose. It matters not that we will soon expire for we may rejoice in having found one another and in the knowledge that we will find one another again when next we incarnate. It is likely that your fear will prevent you from believing this truth. Our time together has been brief. Next time we will have longer. We will challenge your fear until it has no place to reside within you.

'We're going to die,' Theroux whispered, his whole body convulsing. 'We're going to dry out and shrivel up like pieces of fruit, and the vultures will take pieces of us until we're just two skeletons lying in a desert.' He crawled closer to Captive-no-longer and curled up between his legs. *I should have let them shoot you when you were in that hole, it would have been kinder. Then neither of us would be suffering now.*

I suffer not. I have released my hold upon my body so it can expire as it will. I will leave this incarnation feeling full of joy and accomplishment. You could too. All you need do is leave your body and come with me.

That can't be true. I wouldn't be able to hear you in my head if you weren't here anymore. That's if I ever heard you, and I wasn't hallucinating from the start. I'm going to die; this is the end for me.

There is no end and no beginning. We are part of All That Is. We can no more cease to be a part of it than you and I can now cease to be part of one another. Leave your body and come with me. You need not suffer.

Chapter Eight

I need to stay here as long as I can. I need to make the most of each moment because after that there will be no more moments.

That is not the truth. I will remain with you until your body expires and then we will leave together.

Theroux's fear made him hold on to his body through the remainder of the light, through the darkness and into the following light, before, despite every effort to terrify him into finding a last scrap of strength, it could not panic him into keeping his heart beating any longer. It writhed its way throughout Theroux's soul, so that when there was no life left in his body to which his soul could cling and he was forced to flee, the fear left with him.

Captive-no-longer surrounded him with the energy of his heart, holding him together tightly so he could not dissipate as his fear yet convinced him he would.

I am here with you. All is well. Captive-no-longer's assurance was carried throughout Theroux's soul by the energy of his heart. Theroux's fear shrank from it, turning in on itself until it was but the tiniest part of him.

He felt a sense of calm, of rightness, of returning home – just as he had every other time his aged soul had left an incarnation. He also felt the same frustration that had accompanied his most recent returns to All That Is. *Dammit! I've done it AGAIN. How is it that I just can't seem to remember there's no such thing as death? I really thought I'd do it this time – I had enough sensitivity and empathy to risk my life for others, and I was sure that would be enough to help me accept my death when it came, but no, I still behaved like a soul incarnating for the first time. I even had you there telling me the truth, and I still couldn't believe it!*

My influence was not sufficiently prolonged. Next time it will be.

They created no more thoughts for they had no need. They

celebrated their meeting, their bond and their agreement to reincarnate together. They were drawn to those of us who would reincarnate alongside them with shared purpose and intent, and celebrated further with us all for a while. When they peeled away from us Horses Of The New Dawn and our soulmates in order to reincarnate, they did so with the barely controlled enthusiasm for which they would be well known in their lives as Justin and Gas.

I immediately followed Justin and Gas through their current incarnation, observing that Gas's experience of carrying a rider while his body was immature in his last incarnation caused him to wait until his body was strong and mature before calling for his human partner this time around. I reaffirmed my determination to hold Walks A Straight Path away from me until I too was strong enough. I also observed, and was pleased by, the instant affinity Gas and Justin had for one another upon meeting, due to having established their bond in their previous incarnation; I would expect the same when Walks A Straight Path and I were reunited.

By the time they arrived at the location where we had agreed our mission would begin – known to the humans as The Gathering – I found the pair utterly dedicated to their agreement to challenge the outlook and habits that humans tended to find comfortable. I paused my rapid assimilation of their experiences to observe more closely an altercation that seemed to roar with significance.

'Gas isn't happy with what we're asking him to do, Feryl, I'm getting off.'

'We're only asking him to walk forward in a straight line, Justin. All horses find it strange carrying a rider to begin with; you just need to keep your position so you don't get in his way, and then ask him again.'

Chapter Eight

'I've asked him twice now and both times, he's not only refused, but he's felt like he's going to explode. He's in such a state that he can't even tell me what the problem is. Are you going to tell me that's normal too?'

'There's very little about you and Gas that's normal, but that doesn't mean my knowledge and experience aren't sound and as applicable to the two of you as to everyone else. I would remind you that I'm not the Master of Riding for nothing, and you'll do well to follow my instructions.'

Justin leant forward and swung a hind limb over Gas's back before jumping down to the ground. 'Not today; Gas has had enough. Maybe he'll be able to tell me what the problem is once he's calmed down, and we can try again tomorrow.'

I sensed that being ridden was compromising Gas's balance, strength and power. I also sensed that his refusal to enlighten his Bond-Partner as to the problem had nothing to do with his agitated state; he had discovered that there was merit in leaving his Bond-Partner in a quandary so that the human mind might give way to the voice of his soul. I felt immense satisfaction at that which I had gleaned from his experiences.

Chapter Nine

I passed my Woeful test today! Finally! It would have to be Robbie who was stalking me, wouldn't it, and of course he had to make the whole thing into a huge joke and scare me half to death, but at least I've done it. Now I can leave the village on my own to find new herbs to test for the ailments I haven't got cures for yet, and when my horse calls for me, I'll be able to go to her. I'm so excited!

Diary of Amarilla Nixon, aged 14½

I GRAZED alongside my dam as I waited for the voice of my soul to identify which of the Horses Of The New Dawn I should learn from next. I was frustrated by it instead guiding my attention to my body's need for rest, in direct opposition to my mind's desire to forge ahead and continue my education. I was desperate to learn what I could from those who shared my purpose but had been incarnate longer than I, so that I would be as prepared as possible for my life with Walks A Straight path.

Chapter Nine

My dam edged closer and made the same gentle, low sound in her throat that she had when I was little. She knew how tired my body was as a result of our herd's recent migration across the plains, and she knew how tired my mind was due to part of it diverting to learning whilst the rest remained focused on survival. She would stand over me while I slept.

I sensed Walks A Straight Path protesting against her own dam's insistence that she rest in order to relieve pain in her head caused by her own intensive period of learning, and immediately pulled my mind further away from hers; our shared circumstance was causing our minds to resonate even more strongly than normal, and if her anger at her dam were to decrease even slightly, she would notice. She would be unable to resist flooding down the thread that linked us, and I had no doubt that our current resonance would shatter the boundary that I had put in place and she had thus far respected. She would be able to sense where I was in relation to her, and she would come to me before it was time.

My weariness had resulted in a lapse in concentration that could have hindered Walks A Straight Path and me in achieving our objective. My dam was right. I should rest. I refused even to wonder whether Walks A Straight Path had come to a similar realisation.

My dam's shrieks woke me, and the pounding of many feet shaking the earth got me up from the ground. Danger approached; awareness of it rippled through the herd. Instinct allowed me no time for thought – when my dam ran, I was close behind her.

Many in our herd were taller and stronger than I, but none were as determined. I trusted my dam to lead us to safety, and I would stay on her heels until we reached it. Nothing would keep me from surviving long enough to meet Walks A Straight Path when the time came.

Our flight across the plains was difficult, since we ran directly towards the newly appeared light provider. My dam was experienced and wise – our pursuers were forced to run even blinder than we, for where our eyes were on either side of our head, theirs faced directly front. Not only that, but we could run at speed for longer than they, so if they were to bring one of us down, they would need to do it soon. Their howls of frustration signalled their realisation that their hunger was greater than their hunting capability in this instance.

My dam kept running. She would take us well beyond the reach of the fanged ones and then keep us moving at a slower speed until we were outside their territory. She would not risk them following our scent at their leisure and then ambushing us when next they would feed. The energy of the herd shifted from the strongest to the weakest so that they would have the strength to keep pace with the rest of us. I felt a surge of satisfaction that energy shifted from, rather than to, me; my body had gained sufficient strength that for the first time during flight, I was a contributor to the herd's energy rather than a recipient. My body was maturing slower than my mind, but it was maturing.

The heat provider was directly above us when we scented the water for which we were all desperate. My dam led us straight to it and then relaxed the hold upon us that she had employed to ensure that even the weakest continued to follow her across the plains, come what may. We spread ourselves along the edge of the fast-flowing water that ran shallow enough at its edges not to be a danger to the youngest among us, and drew it into our bodies until we could contain no more. Then we pulled at stalks of grass as we made our way towards the shade providers, who, despite holding most of their nutrition out of our reach, we nevertheless valued for the shelter they gave us from the heat provider.

As always, my dam had shown her experience. We had scented water twice during our flight, but the first was within the territory of those who had hunted us, and the second was far from shade or a reliable source of nutrition. She had brought us to a place we could rest and recover the energy of the herd.

I sensed her weariness as she reached the shade that I had already spent some time enjoying. Since I was now a contributor to the energy of the herd, I felt confident enough to approach her with the intention of watching over her while she slept. She flicked her ears backward, expressing her rejection of my offer; she was my dam and it was her job to watch over me. I didn't slow my curved approach towards her shoulder. When I reached her, I locked my forelimbs in place and rested a hind limb. I would rest my body whilst remaining alert for any sign of danger to the herd, so that she could sleep.

She recognised the determination within me that I had honed whilst still in her belly, and I sensed the trust she had in its strength. She considered my intention; I was not attempting to supplant her as our matriarch, for I still planned to leave the herd when the time was right. I merely recognised her need to rest and would watch over her as she always had for me.

My dam folded her forelimbs and lowered her body to the ground with a thump. Dead nutrition that had fallen from those now shading us cushioned and supported her tired body. Her concern for her herd fell away from her as her trust in me facilitated her retreat from the waking world. The rest of the herd sensed her sinking into a deep slumber, and, one by one, followed her lead as they did in everything else, until I alone stood watch.

I was trusted in my dam's stead. They knew I was strong enough, shrewd enough and sensitive enough to sense potential danger in the environment that was, for our kind, one of the most dangerous due to the Sorrowful, and act for the good of the herd before it became imminent. If my herd could trust me with their survival, then so would Walks A Straight Path be able to when the situation called for it. Satisfaction hummed through my body.

At the thought of my soulmate, my attention flickered briefly to the other Horses Of The New Dawn, from whose experience I was still desperate to learn in order to prepare myself. I immediately pulled it back so that I could devote it entirely to my awareness of my environment, and to interpreting the information provided by my physical senses. I would ensure that the trust of my herd was well placed.

It wasn't until darkness replaced the light that my dam emerged from her slumber. I was gratified to sense that where she had been overcome by weariness, now her usual vigilance, acumen and wisdom had regained prominence in its stead.

She assessed our current situation – many of our number still slept, but a few had begun pulling at the grass whose sweet scent promised a higher level of contentment than we had been used to of late – by the time she was standing on her feet. She sensed my opinion regarding the current level of risk to the herd – minimal, the only slight danger being if the dams of the youngest members of our herd should be distracted and not notice their offspring straying too close to the fast-moving water.

My dam not only concurred with my appraisal, but approved

Chapter Nine

of my watchfulness over two youngsters celebrating their newly gained wakefulness by chasing one another closer to the water whilst their dams grazed furiously, intent on nourishing themselves sufficiently that they could in turn nourish their young.

My dam nudged my awareness. She would resume her duties as our matriarch. I could rest.

I followed her away from the soft dampness of the shade providers to the hard, cracked ground from which sprouted the grass. I pulled at it until my body's cravings subsided, then drew in water before lying down just close enough to its flowing body that I could continue to benefit from its coolness.

My body was satiated, I was comfortable, and I was surrounded by those whose wakefulness ensured I could sleep. Further, I had begun to fulfil the potential my herd had perceived in me when I was born. My contentment eased me into a deep sleep from which I emerged full of determination to resume my learning.

I reached out to the other Horses before I was even on my feet. As I snatched at the first stalks of grass, I resonated most closely with the one who was performing the same activity.

I would learn next from the male who was now known as Oak.

Chapter Ten

NOTICE TO QUARRY EMPLOYEES
Each cart is now to make four trips per day to the quarry.
If any loads fall short, or any carts are not back at the yard with
their last load by sundown, the drivers of those carts will be fined.
The Guvnor

WHERE GAS HAD INCARNATED few times previously, Oak was an old and experienced soul. Having lived so many lives as so many different species, he had reached a level of evolution and understanding that made it inevitable he would incarnate this time as one of us. As such, he had not chosen a tranquil existence in his previous incarnation; in order to attract the human with the strength, courage and compassion he sought, he had been willing to endure suffering in the extreme.

His dam had been exhausted by the time his body signalled to hers that he was ready to enter the cruel world in which she lived. She sensed the age and wisdom present in her unborn offspring.

Chapter Ten

She knew of his intention to find light in the darkness. She took strength from that intention and combined it with the small amount offered to her by those of our kind who worked alongside her and were equally exhausted, yet sensed that her need for strength was greater than theirs.

Despite her neglected and abused condition, she endured her labour and produced a foal who was stronger and healthier than should have been possible. The reason for his vitality became clear when she collapsed soon after her return to harness, whilst pulling a vessel heaped high with the pieces chipped out of the ground that humans deemed valuable; she had funnelled everything of herself into him in order that he might survive to achieve his aim.

Her youngster shrieked at her to get up. He skipped around her on ungainly limbs, desperate for her to rise.

'Stupid old nag's had it, I reckon,' said a harsh voice. 'Get her foal out of the way while I check.'

Thin strips of dried animal skin cracked the air, and the youngster moved away from his dam, his ears quivering and his sides heaving with distress. A female in the line of vessels behind his dam made a low noise in her throat, trying to reassure the foal, but all he could think of was getting back near his dam. Besides his instinct to remain at her side, his belly was warning him of his need for her.

'Yep, she's had it. That's gonna set you two behind schedule. Braxton, get that harness off her. Fielding, go back to the stables and fetch another nag to take her place.' The owner of the voice climbed onto the vessel and shouted, 'The rest of you, go around this mess, you know what'll happen if you're late getting that slate back to the yard.'

'What about the foal, Guvnor?' Braxton asked.

'Let him get back to his ma, then when he tries to suckle, truss him up and chuck him on the wagon. We'll take him back to the yard and the missus can keep him alive until I'm ready for him.'

"The missus" was too scared of her mate to do anything but keep the youngster alive. She fed him suckling fluid from a vessel that mimicked his dam's teat, and shut the door of his stall before each period of darkness so that he would stay warm. Yet despite being a dam herself, she ignored his cries for his own dam with ease. She also neglected the wounds on his limbs from where they had been tied together in order to transport him, so that they attracted tormentors and disease. It was only when his rapidly weakening state forced her to, that she cleaned his wounds and applied a healing mixture to them, lest her mate beat her.

Once he was feeling stronger, she allowed her children to throw missiles at him, causing him to run around his small enclosure until his fur was wet with cooling fluid and he could run no more.

Neither his pain and confusion at being alone and without his dam to nurture and protect him, nor the misery caused him by the humans at every opportunity, could deter him from his course. He would not give up on life. He would endure. When those who externalised their own pain and fear by tormenting him realised their mistake, whether in this incarnation or another, their horror would fuel their need for self-improvement, for thus operates the mechanism of balance. He would aid them in their process of self-discovery whilst waiting for the one who was already far in advance of them.

He stuck fast to his resolve when the "guvnor" deemed him big enough to be trained to "pull his weight", which, it transpired, was meant literally. To begin with, they tied his limbs together, as they had when taking him from his dam. When he couldn't move, they tied his head to the cord holding his forelimbs together and pulled it, so that his head was forced downward and anchored there. They felt no compassion for him as they put his dam's harness around his neck and torso and tightened it to fit, regardless of his terrified grunts and struggles.

They laughed as he tried to escape his bindings, and guessed at how long it would be before he ceased his efforts. It was only when he finally did that they removed everything that was confining him, and left him be. Exhausted, he lay down where he was and heeded the voice of his soul as it reminded him why he was there and of the purpose he was serving to his abusers and himself.

When darkness gave way to light, he was subjected to the same treatment. Try as he might, he could not escape the cords they threw to trap and bind his limbs, and he could not prevent them from tightening the harness around his neck and torso. He ceased his struggles sooner than the first time.

It was only when, after many incidents of the same treatment, he lost the will to struggle at all, that they ceased tying him down and instead forced something sharp into his mouth, held in place by strappings around his head. While he was tossing his head around, trying to dislodge it, dried strips of animal skin lashed down on his back, causing him to jump forward… until something jerked him to a stop; the harness was attached to a vessel that his young body could not possibly move.

'Unload it, you daft bugger. He can't pull that amount yet, look at him, he's still got his foal's tail,' a voice yelled, laden not with compassion but with humour.

There was shifting and grunting behind him, but he couldn't find the will to turn his head to see what was causing the noise. When the strips of skin lashed at him once more, causing him to jump forward again, the vessel to which he was harnessed shifted behind him. He was lashed again before he could think of stopping, and as he leant into the harness, the vessel kept pace with him. Several voices cheered at the fact that he had been broken to the will of humans.

An insistent, sharp tug on his mouth had him staggering to a stop. He had barely registered the pain in his mouth when the lash ensured his forward movement again. A harsh tug on one side of his mouth almost caused him to fall as his limbs scrambled to follow the new direction in which his head had been hauled. The humans laughed at his ungainly manoeuvring, not one of them concerned by the life fluid now dripping from his mouth.

'Turn him the other way. Let's see if he can stay on those wobbly legs again,' called a voice laced with cruel anticipation. Its owner radiated the misery with which he had been raised, as well as his inherited need to expel it by inflicting it on those around him.

By the time the humans had finished tormenting their quarry, he could no longer stand. He was relieved of his harness whilst lying on the ground.

'Like mother, like son,' the guvnor said, standing over him and shaking his head. 'You're going to need to find a bit more strength, lad, or you'll last barely longer than she did.' He turned to one of the other humans. 'Feed him extra now he's going to be working, we need every last bit out of him before he follows his ma.'

He came to realise that the light brought with it pain and exhaustion, and seemed to last forever, and that the darkness allowed rest and a little nourishment for his body, but was over far

Chapter Ten

too quickly. The only thing of which he could be certain as his body slowly crumbled under the weight of his loads, was that the light's ability to follow the darkness was relentless.

He shouldn't have survived as long as he did; any other of our kind would have released their hold on their body long before. But the opportunity to improve the balance of both our kind and humankind called to him as strongly as the imbalance to which he was currently being subjected highlighted its necessity. He knew he wouldn't fail; the balance of life would ensure it.

Even so, he was nearing the end of his body's scant reserves as he pulled his vessel along the track to the quarry whilst suffering a particularly harsh beating from the heat provider as well as from the strips of animal skin held by one of his drivers. The others of our kind had long since left him behind, their mature bodies responding more vigorously to their beating than could his.

'We won't suffer the lash just because we got landed with your puny little hide today,' said the driver who was beating him. The lash cracked through the air and landed on an existing wound, but he barely flinched, and increased his pace not at all.

When a shadow darkened the path in front of him, he dared not balk from it or stop, for fear of his torn mouth being hauled upon to steer him back on track, or the lash descending yet again.

His mouth was further assaulted regardless, as he was pulled to a sharp halt. He inhaled the scent of an unfamiliar human. His dull eyes vaguely registered a slightly built, middle-aged female, even as his awareness registered exactly who she was.

Chapter Eleven

NOTICE TO QUARRY EMPLOYEES
Anyone caught feeding the horses more than their
allotted amount will receive ten lashes.
The Guvnor

'WELL, now I've seen it all.' Her voice was sharp with rage, yet softened at its edges by her compassion for the abused soul before her. 'Not content with working adult horses to death, you've sunk even lower to using foals? What is he? Eighteen months old?'

'Get outta our way, woman, we're already running behind. Unless you fancy a more enjoyable diversion? Now that would be worth suffering a fine for, wouldn't it, Deakin?' The vessel behind me creaked as the male who had spoken stepped down off it, onto the ground.

The female experienced a flash of fear before channelling it into her existing rage. 'You think you can take me, do you?' she

Chapter Eleven

said, drawing an implement from a cord around her waist and pointing it at him. 'You and whose army?'

The male stepped backward even as his companion howled with mirth.

'You,' the female said, pointing her implement towards the male who remained atop the vessel. 'Throw that horsewhip down here to me.' The howling stopped. 'Now.'

'Now look here, we're just doing our job, there's no need for any nastiness,' said the male on the ground.

'I think that ship has sailed, don't you?' the female human replied through her teeth. 'Look at the state of this baby. BABY! He's a starving baby horse, and you've been beating him near to death.' She looked back up at the other male. 'Throw down the whip or I'll shoot you where you sit.' She moved something on the implement with a click. The lash landed at her feet with no further argument. 'Right, get down here, and the two of you take off your shirts and kneel on the ground.' There was a pause. 'I won't ask you twice.'

The males did as they were bid. They stank of fear.

'Move and I'll shoot you,' the female said. 'Make any noise as the whip lands on your back, and I'll do it again until you learn to suffer in silence, just like you've made this poor baby do.'

'Our guvnor'll have your hide for this,' growled one of the males.

'Your guvnor knows I have evidence that he's been embezzling money from the owners of this disgusting company, and that if anything happens to me, it'll find its way to those who won't hesitate to use it. I may have not long moved to this valley, but I've made it my business to find ways to make sure everyone leaves me alone.'

There was a scream as the lash landed across the back of the male who had spoken, then another as the other male felt its bite.

'How many times have you used this vile weapon? Huh?' There were more screams. 'How many horses have suffered at your hands, you despicable excuses for human beings?' The lash cracked again. 'Did you ever wonder how it feels to be horsewhipped? Well, now you know.' Screams rang through the air again.

'Stop, please, stop,' one of the males pleaded.

'You know how to make me stop. Suffer in silence, like you've made countless horses do. And don't you dare faint on me, because I have a message I need you to pass on to your guvnor.'

When the lash sounded again, there was a barely audible grunt. The next crack was met with silence. There was a pause and then a snapping noise before the lash landed between the males in pieces.

'You won't be using that to hurt any horse, ever again,' the female said. She threw a pouch onto the ground atop the ruined implement. 'This poor foal is almost done. That there is what he's worth to the meat man. You'll give it to your guvnor and tell him that Pixie took a dead foal off your hands, fair and square. You'll also tell him that the horses in his charge will be fed, watered and rested sufficiently that they can pull their loads without needing to be horsewhipped in order to keep them moving. He won't see me, but I'll be watching, and if he wants the evidence I have against him to stay buried, he'll stop this abuse. Got it?'

'How are we supposed to tell him that when he'll kill us for knowing he's cheating the quarry owners?' one of the males asked in between short, sharp breaths.

There was a pause before Pixie replied, 'Tell him you're both under my protection too. Should either of you fall foul of any accident, the evidence will surface.'

'This is what you call being under your protection?' the other male asked, pointing a limb at his own back.

Chapter Eleven

'That's what's known as justice,' Pixie said. 'Just because you can take your misery out on defenceless animals, it doesn't mean you should. Now, I'm done with you two. I'm guessing neither of you wants it known that you got beaten by a woman, so I suggest you put your shirts back on and get yourselves back to the yard, full of how you just got a load of money for a dead foal.'

One of the males stood up. 'How about we just tell the guvnor exactly what happened here, leaving out any mention of his cheating and your threat?'

'Then the appalling treatment of his horses will continue, I'll see it and take him down, and he'll be murdered in his sleep – as will his employees for being complicit.'

The males considered her declaration whilst carefully, painfully, replacing their garments.

'You have a deal,' one of them said quietly, staring at her with hate in his eyes.

'I didn't offer you a deal, I threatened you,' Pixie said, 'and you've just realised you have no choice but to do as I say. Now, get yourselves gone.' She waved the implement at them of which they were so fearful.

They stepped backward hastily, almost falling over, then turned and hurried away. Pixie watched them until they were too far away to cause her harm, then turned back to he who had been waiting his whole miserable life for her.

'It's alright now, beautiful boy, you're coming home with me and nobody's ever going to hurt you again,' she told him softly. 'I'm going to call you Dewr. It means brave.'

She loosened the harness whilst he stood with his head drooping, his nose almost on the ground. Then she slowly removed it, strap by strap, talking to him all the while. 'You poor soul, look at you, you're covered in wounds and scars. They've been working you for a while, haven't they? Your body looks all wrong. Look how strong you are though, to have survived everything they've done to you. Now, I'm going to tie this rope around your neck, just so I have a way to help you understand to stay next to me while I get you away from here. Just open your mouth for me now, so I can get that wire out.' He understood her intention and parted his jaws. 'You absolute sweetheart. You understand me, don't you? I'm not sure how, but I can kind of feel you can. I'm just going to loop the rope around your nose so I can guide you more easily, is that alright?'

Dewr lifted his head with difficulty and explored Pixie's eyes with his own as she knotted the rope in place. They immediately filled with fluid that spilled down her face. She rubbed the side of his face so gently he could barely feel it. 'You're so broken on the outside, but you're so strong on the inside. Why do I get the feeling that it isn't me who's rescuing you, but the other way around?' Her forelimb trembled as his eyes continued to reach and soothe the part of her she had buried since fleeing her abusive herd.

She jumped as a lash cracked in the distance. 'Come on, my brave one, we need to leave; no one other than those two morons can know you're still alive.' Her breath caught in her throat as Dewr turned to walk alongside her with no pressure on the rope. 'Your feet and legs are so sore, I'm so sorry to make you do this.'

Dewr picked up his ungainly pace a little, confirming to Pixie that her feeling about him was correct – that while he may be sore and broken, wherever she went, he would walk by her side.

Pixie went on to provide the two of them with a peaceful life, full of love and companionship. But in isolating them from other humans, she also isolated them from any opportunity to clear their souls of the burdens of abuse inflicted on Dewr by the quarry workers, and on Pixie by her herd.

When they eventually left their lives behind, Dewr was gentle in helping Pixie to realise her mistake. As soon as she did, her soul wove its way regretfully around Dewr's.

I'm sorry. I thought I was doing the right thing.

Regret is unnecessary. We both carry the weight of unresolved pain. The bond we have developed will give us the strength to shed it when next we incarnate and in so doing we will contribute to the evolution of both our kinds. You will experience more difficulty than I but do not fear for I will be the sanctuary for you in our next life together that you were for me in this.

Immediately, their thoughts drew them to the rest of us who shared their mission, but they did not rejoice with us for long. I followed Pixie's essence as she hurled herself into the life she would need to live in order to fulfil her Bond-Partner's vision for them both.

As Rowena, she thrashed her way through a difficult childhood and adolescence, the pain of being neglected by her dam compounded by that which she had brought with her from her life as Pixie. She retained all Pixie's feistiness and willingness to protect those not as strong or confident as she, and it transpired that excess pain combined with a fierce personality was a volatile mixture, tempered only by her incalculable devotion to the soul whom she had no memory of rescuing in her last incarnation.

He whom she had previously named Dewr was now known to her as Oak, and he was as much the calm to her storm as he had promised he would be. I was fascinated by the approach I sensed him taking to guide his partner towards balance, despite her ingrained pattern of fighting the world from a place of pain.

Patience. He had trusted the bond he would have with his partner while it was still an idea, and he'd had the forbearance to endure extreme suffering in his previous incarnation whilst he waited for it to become a reality. He had been content to live an entire lifetime strengthening it in preparation for that which it would need to endure, and now that it hummed with the energy of both their hearts, he knew it was invincible. Whatever befell Rowena and Oak, however challenging the circumstances both externally and between the two of them, their bond would hold them together whilst he accompanied her on her journey. He merely needed to be all that he already was to her… and wait.

I absorbed Oak's patience, noting as I did so that it settled less easily within me than in him, and to a far lesser extent. Because his role differed from mine. His partner differed from mine. Where it was necessary for patience and strength to be his overriding characteristics, it was essential that focus and determination were mine. The Horses Of The New Dawn would all bring different strengths to our mission so that in our entirety, we would bring balance. Nevertheless, I appreciated the additional patience and endurance that now resided within me as a result of experiencing life through he who was now Oak.

I wandered over to the body of water that continued to rush past my herd as if overdue for being somewhere else. I savoured its crisp scent, almost tasting it in my dry, grass-lined mouth before reaching it. When I had drunk my fill, I felt restless. I would play.

I jumped up the low bank to where the long grass waved lazily in the warm breeze, and leapt into the air, forelimbs followed by hind limbs, with a loud squeal. I kicked my hind limbs out behind me on landing and then tore past those who were grazing, biting one another in friendship or standing head to tail at rest so that they could dislodge biters from one another.

The oldest members of our herd ignored my antics, but the rest acknowledged and approved of my exuberance with a range of reactions, from a small leap of their own, to a raised head or the flick of an ear. Some of them came tearing after me, as I knew they would. Yet as they chased me, I sensed their perception of me shifting. Where they would normally have chased me without reservation until I stopped and spun around, inviting one or more of them to mimic my leaps and bounds before we all ran after whomever took the lead next, on this occasion there was a hesitancy in those following me. I immediately perceived why.

As members of the same herd, we generally operated as one; our actions were driven by a shared perception of ourselves as a single entity, with the energy of the herd available to all and flowing wherever it was needed. We all had different strengths and weaknesses, but since we were all parts of the same whole, those differences complemented each other, often cancelling one another out. I was differentiating myself from the herd consciousness with my learning; I was becoming more of an individual, and they weren't sure how to relate to me.

I felt a flicker of fear. To give myself the best chance of survival, I needed to remain part of the herd until it was time to leave to find Walks A Straight Path; I couldn't risk becoming so different from them, so far apart from the herd mentality, that they rejected me. Yet I needed to learn, to develop myself further so that when that time came, I would be robust enough to meet the challenge I knew I would face.

As those who had followed me faltered and began to peel away from our game, I resonated acutely with one of the other Horses Of The New Dawn – one who was in an identical position to me and had learnt how to negotiate the challenge. Without hesitation, I absorbed the experience of she who would be Flame and made it part of me.

Chapter Twelve

Witch – A woman with knowledge or skills feared by men.

Definition added to the Histories of The New by
Keeper Lorenda Butler

SHE WHO WOULD BE Flame carried the same level of determination as did I, the same resolve to do as she had agreed to do before incarnating, and the same acceptance of the fact that in so doing, she would face one of the biggest challenges her soul had faced in any of its incarnations. Like me, she knew she must prepare herself if she were to succeed; she must take herself beyond the learning and experiences of her herd.

Like my herd, the members of hers were different expressions of the same consciousness, largely responding to one another by feel and instinct, and accepting their places in the hierarchy so that the herd functioned as one body composed of all its co-operating parts. Only when the hormones of young males caused their behaviour to set them apart were they turned away to form their

Chapter Twelve

own herds. Only when breeding females were imminently due to give birth did they take themselves away from the herd without their actions causing ripples of unease to those whose survival depended upon the herd's cohesion. Only when one became so old or unwell as to slow the flight of the rest from danger were they left behind.

So, how was she who would be Flame managing to spend time apart from her herd in order to familiarise herself with the unease of doing so? How was she finding ways to practise coping with the fear of isolation so ingrained in all of our kind, without that fear affecting her herd? I immediately grasped why she was doing so – her soul knew that when the time came, she would never cope with being by herself whilst severely injured if she didn't first learn to cope with being by herself whilst healthy. So, she listened to its voice as it advised her to go against her instinct to remain with her herd.

But how was she doing it? By infusing her herd with the energy of her heart to the extent that they weren't capable of mustering concern for her or themselves during her absences; by cocooning them in it to the point that their sense of wellbeing over-rode both their and her sense of vulnerability. The warmth of her heart was sufficient to maintain her place in the herd regardless of her divergent behaviour and strength.

The energy of her heart was immense because her previous incarnation had ensured it would be.

She had been male then, and the companion of a female human – a healer. The two of them travelled between human settlements, he pulling into his harness from first light to last in order that they would travel the dangerous tracks as quickly as possible, she trading her skills for the healing supplies and nourishment that would keep them both alive.

He knew she valued him above all else, even her own life, for she didn't believe her life was worth living without him. She checked his body daily and, if necessary, used her healing supplies on him before sparing any thought for what she would need for herself or those to whom she would tend at the next settlement.

While she healed her fellow humans, she didn't like them; they were violent and untrustworthy. They may have treated her with respect whilst surrounded by other humans who would bear witness in the settlements, but she, her possessions and he who pulled her vessel were prey to them whilst travelling alone.

Despite the dangers of travelling, it was only when they had left humans behind and there was just the two of them that she felt calm and at peace. When darkness replaced light and they pulled off the track to rest, she would allow the sounds of him grazing and moving around to soothe her to sleep. She never slept for the duration of the darkness; her body was attuned enough to his to wake when he in turn needed to sleep. She would take to her feet as her way of assuring him that she would now take over being alert for danger so that he could truly rest.

Whenever they were ambushed by humans on the tracks between villages, she would undo the straps that she had incorporated into his harness so that it could instantly fall away from him. It was only on those occasions that she took the lash from its holder on her vessel and dropped it upon his hind end, with the intention that he would flee the scene and continue running until he was safe. Her terror at the treatment she would endure from her attackers was always overwhelmed by the energy of her heart that she sent after him in order to help him on his way.

She never allowed herself to hope that he would return to her after his instinct to flee had been satisfied, but he always did; the energy of her heart swelled his to the point that he yearned to

Chapter Twelve

return it in a way she would understand. He would find her abused in the ways of which only humans were capable, and robbed of anything that the "bandits", as she called them, deemed valuable. In his absence, the bandits had no way of taking her vessel, and no interest in her healing supplies or his nutrition, but they took everything else.

Regardless of her condition – even on occasions when she had been beaten senseless – his return would rouse both her body and her intention to continue living, and she would pile dried grass from the cart onto the ground for him to eat whilst she checked his body for injury. The energy of her heart greeted his, refusing merely to take it but rather entwining it with her own so that it could only grow.

Only when she was satisfied that his needs had been met would she tend to her own. She was tough in terms of the amount of abuse she could endure, yet sensitive to an extent of which other humans of her time could not conceive. She knew that success was not measured by possessions or the number of humans one had forced into subservience, but by the ability to see beauty in her surroundings, regardless of location; to revel in the touch of the givers of life that were the heat provider and the drops of fluid that fell from the sky; to know how it felt to love and be loved.

The human way of referring to the energy of the heart took nothing away from its truth. She felt it from him as intensely as she returned it, and it sustained her through all the tribulations of interacting with her own kind. She healed them with kindness and compassion despite knowing that, given the chance, they would rob her of her possessions, her dignity and her health.

Following repeated visits to one particular settlement, the male humans who claimed authority over the rest began to resent the number of residents flocking to see her. He who loved her sensed their fear of her ability to provide a skill that they could not. They saw it as a challenge to their leadership. They told themselves and those who sought her out that her ability to provide healing was unnatural, and that anyone who consorted with her was guilty of consorting with darkness.

She never doubted herself, even when she saw the faces of those in the settlement turning from hopeful to hateful. How could she, when she felt the truth from him in every moment of every day. Even so, she would have left the settlement were it not for a youngster whom she had tended on her previous visits, and whose progress she was keen to assess. She endured the taunts and sneers of those surrounding her vessel as she stood upon it, watching for the youngster who pulled at her mind. As the crowd of fearful humans increased in size with no sign of the youngster or his dam, she finally conceded that the humans of the settlement were beyond her help.

With a long outward breath, she sat down on her vessel and signalled to he who stood patiently in his harness that it was time for them to leave.

The humans gathered in front of him, blocking his way.

'Where do you think you're going, Witch?' a male shouted. Those around him echoed his words as they pushed one another to get closer to her.

'My services are clearly not wanted here anymore, so I'm doing as you all seem to want me to, and leaving,' she said, her voice clear and true. 'Please move out of Gabe's way, and we'll be gone. You'll never see us again.'

'Let you leave, so you can take your dark ways to other God-fearing settlements?'

She turned to see who had spoken, and her eyes came to rest

Chapter Twelve

upon the leaders of the settlement, mounted upon those of our kind whom they had broken in both body and mind. She drew in a sharp breath and stood back up on her vessel. 'Oh, your poor horses. At least let me help them before I go?'

'Help them?' one of the males said. 'Curse them, you mean. Before we know it, they'll be full of your venom and either throwing us or dying horrible deaths.' He looked around at the crowd, nodding with satisfaction as they raised their forelimbs and shouted their agreement.

She was full of sadness as she sat back down, but she sent the energy of her heart to those of our kind she could not help, before exchanging more of it with Gabe as he stood waiting to take her away from those who now feared her. When they began kicking his legs in order to punish her, fear settled into each and every one of his wounds.

'NO!' she screamed. She pulled the straps that allowed his harness to fall away from him and jumped down from her vessel, lash in hand. Never before had she raised it to another human, but now she set about all those who hurt Gabe – not out of fear of them but out of love for him. She would set him free and send him away from danger as she had so many times before.

She surprised them with her actions and scared them with her ferocity. They moved away uncertainly, shielding their faces from her lash. She dropped it upon Gabe's wide, strong hindquarters, sending the energy of her heart with it to ease the pain and shock of her action, as she had so many times before.

'Go, Gabe, go!' Her intention combined with her intense desire that he be safe, fuelling the flight instinct with which he had been battling. He fled, his sturdy legs sore and bleeding but well able to carry him away from the insanity surrounding her.

The energy of her heart followed him, pushing him further and further away, even as it held the hate of the humans away from her so that she didn't succumb to their madness.

When they tied her to her vessel, lashed her until she was almost senseless, and then created flames beneath her, she tried to focus on her memories of her life with Gabe and her overwhelming love for him, instead of on her pain and fear. As she left her burning body, she gave him all she had left, hoping that it would sustain him while he healed and that he would live out the rest of his life away from humans and their vitriol.

When she was free of her incarnation, he was there to help her process it and adjust to existence beyond the veil that souls pull down to blind them when they enter a human body. It didn't take her long to remember herself as a soul who had incarnated many times.

She was pleased with her achievement in her most recent incarnation – despite not being consciously aware of her true nature as part of All That Is, she had acted as if she were. She had lived her life in her own peaceful way, refusing to succumb to the fearful existence chosen by most other humans of the time. She had treated them with compassion regardless of how they treated her, for they were but children who would learn by their mistakes. Many of them had learnt from her, whether they realised it or not, for they could not help but be affected by the energy of her heart, and would recognise its touch when they felt it again. She had trusted the voice of her soul to guide her actions and feelings, despite it being a whisper where to our kind it was a roar.

She was ecstatic to remember her oneness with Gabe and All That Is. She was relieved that the part of him that was incarnate was beyond the reach of humans and free of serious injury, but she was concerned that his physical wounds were imbued with fear; they would heal to an extent, but would break open at the slightest knock or scratch. Free of the restraints that physicality put upon her ability to heal, she threw all of herself into exorcising the fear within his wounds so that he could heal completely and live out his life in peace.

It will not work, he told her. *You know this. Wounds sustained whilst incarnate may only be cleared whilst incarnate.*

She paused her efforts.

The energy of our hearts is substantial as a result of our devotion to one another, he continued. *When next we incarnate together it will draw us together as surely as will the fear that now resides within us both. In using one to overcome the other we will evoke great change. We will contribute to improving the balance of our species and thus the balance of physical existence.*

They felt the pull of those of us who would work alongside them and were instantly with us, celebrating our shared purpose. We rejoiced in the courage and devotion to one another that gave them the strength to commit to the most challenging of roles in our mission. Concern flickered within her at our recognition of the fact.

He was there for her instantly, telling her, *Your love for me acted as your anchor to the truth whilst you were incarnate. It will do so again. We will not fail.*

Her concern vanished and we celebrated anew.

Now that they were incarnate again, he as she who would be Flame and she as a female Sorrowful, their lives were proceeding exactly as they had planned. They were taking every opportunity to remember the extent of their courage. Their capacity to love had not dimmed, but rather lit up the lives of those around them. They had not yet met but when they did, the energy of their hearts would prevail regardless of circumstance, for its power had already influenced me; I would use the energy of my heart to reassure my herd that my differences were nothing to fear, just as she who would be Flame did with hers.

She sensed my delight at having learnt from her, and she strengthened her resolve to be as open to learning from me when the time came. She who would be Flame was formidable indeed.

I turned back to my herd, which the other youngsters had rejoined. I would renew my attempt to entice them to play, and this time I would succeed.

Chapter Thirteen

I discovered today that nettle can ease prickly heat, as well as gout and water retention! It's a superherb! I'm going to spend the next few days seeing if it can ease any other ailments, although I'm running out of space to record everything I know about it on its page in my herb journal. Who knew I could get so excited about something other than horses!

Diary of Amarilla Nixon, aged 15

WHEN THE SHADE providers began to drop their nutrition, our behaviour shifted as it did each time our environment altered in this way; we stood close to one another at rest in order to share warmth, rather than to flick biters from one another. As the growth of grass and herbs slowed, we moved more rapidly between feeding grounds, and, as always, more rapidly still whenever danger approached.

The energy of my heart wove through my herd in a constant

flow, ensuring my continued inclusion in our rituals for survival. When the ground was covered by cold, solid flakes, we dug with our forelimbs and rummaged with our noses to find buried nutrition. When we reached sources of water that yet flowed, I joined the older members of our herd in grinding its slippery edges into the earth so that the youngsters could drink without fear of sliding into its deep, turbulent current.

Though my efforts to reassure my herd that I was still a part of them were continual, it wasn't until the heat provider was strong enough to free the fluid from the influence of the cold, and reveal the nutrition it had long buried, that I felt my acceptance in the herd was back to where it had been before I began learning from the other Horses. Even my dam, who had known I would be different before I assumed the body of her unborn offspring, had taken almost as much time as the rest to reconcile whom I had become with one who still belonged in her herd.

Since I had no sense that it was even close to time to call Walks A Straight Path to me, there was no hurry for me to learn from the remaining Horses. Yet the determination that drove us both caused me to feel restless until the heat provider was once more at its strongest and highest in the expanse above, and I finally felt that my position as a member of the herd was unassailable. It was now as normal for me to immerse the others of my kind in the energy of my heart as it was for me to breathe, and as normal for them to accept it – and me – as it was for them to accept the soothing warmth of the heat provider.

I would learn more.

My efforts to be acceptable to my herd members resonated with the experiences of he who was currently bonded to one human and had taken the unusual step of agreeing to support two more when the time came. All three souls he had agreed to help were those for whom this incarnation would be their last. All three needed only a little help from him, but it would be in the same form each time; he would not only – as did all bonded horses – respond to the aspects of their personality of which it would serve them to be aware, but he would amplify those aspects to the extent that all three humans would fully know themselves and the power they brought to the physical experience.

He who was now Spider, like the rest of our kind who had agreed to partner the bringers of change, had incarnated with his current partner before. Before encountering him in that lifetime, he had been acquired by humans who were impressed by who his dam and sire were, to the extent that they failed to question who he was. They wanted him to jump obstacles as competently and willingly as his sire. They wanted him to be as fast across the ground, whilst remaining as open to instruction, as his dam.

When he refused to jump, they inspected his body. When they could find nothing wrong, they tried different approaches to persuade him to clear the obstacles that were so important to them, none of which persuaded him to comply.

The implement that they strapped to his back in order to aid their own balance and security was restricting the movement of his forelimbs. He felt uneasy about leaving the ground with a rider when he wasn't confident about returning to it due to a lack of strength and balance. Yet neither of those things would have prevented him attempting to carry his rider over an obstacle if that rider were willing to learn from the experience; if they were open to change. Those who sat on his back wanted him to do what they wanted, when they wanted, so they could win the admiration of their peers. They were closed to the opportunities his partnership offered, and as a bringer of balance, he could not help but be closed to their attempts to take him and themselves further away from it.

Their frustration with him turned to anger and then to hate.

Their relief when he allowed himself to be led onto the vessel that would take him away was matched equally by his. But when he arrived at a place where humans behaved in exactly the same way towards him, his relief was replaced by disappointment and dread.

By the time he was collected from his fifth residence and taken to a place where there were many others who had disappointed humans who had welcomed the idea of them, rather than the reality of them as bringers of balance, he was underweight despite having been offered a constant source of nutrition. His coat was dull despite having been groomed with each rise of the heat provider. His eyes were dull and downcast, and he had minimal interest in his surroundings.

When the hind end of the vessel that had collected him from those he had disappointed most recently was lowered to the ground, the air that billowed into it was as heavy with fear as it was sharp with violence. It stabbed at his lungs even as it weighed them down, so that he had to snort in order to expel it.

'What's wrong with his breathing? Don't tell me you've gone and picked up another wrong'un? It'll come out of your wages if you have,' an elderly male human said, staring up at him from the ground as he stood, trembling on the vessel.

A younger male appeared at his side. 'He was fine when I picked him up, probably just a bit of dust from the hay. Here are his papers. With breeding like that, we'll make a return on him in no time.'

The elderly human peered back up at the vessel, suspicion and mistrust radiating off him. 'If it were that easy, he wouldn't be here in the first place, would he, Sean? What reason did they give you for wanting shot of him?'

'Overstocked, they said. She's having a baby, and he needs fewer horses there to take care of on his own. They haven't done much with him even though he's six now. They loose-schooled him over some jumps for me, and he looks like he's got his dad's ability and his mum's trainability, so I think we just got lucky. That's his name, by the way.'

'Lucky?' The older human showed his teeth. 'We'll see. Stick him next to Old Betty; she won't be bothered if he gets a strop on him.' He pointed past a long row of stalls, each confining one of our kind.

Sean sprang up the ramp and led Lucky, still snorting, off the vessel. The human yanked hard on Lucky's head. 'Don't even think of trying anything, you understand me? Walk calmly, and we won't come to blows. Act like a pillock and you'll get my boot in your belly.'

The human stank of fear. Lucky raised his head in order to try to find more comfortable air to breathe, only to have it pulled back down again. He grunted as Sean followed through on his threat and kicked him.

'Try that again and you'll get another,' the human said, his fear increasing. 'You'll soon learn the score around here.'

By the time a young male human wandered onto the residence, looking around himself as if uncertain why he was there, Lucky had indeed learnt how the elderly human and his offspring operated. Their fear of their charges was surpassed only by their certainty that with sufficient violence, they could make them do what they wanted, and by their desperation to pass them on to other humans before they became too distressed for pain-numbing and mind-calming potions to work.

At the sight of a newcomer meandering around, the elderly human put a forelimb out to block his offspring from leaving the room in which they rested, ate and sheltered from inclement weather, and strode out of it himself. 'Well, hello there, young sir. Alfred Bates is the name. And you are?'

'Sol Grantham.'

'Okay, Sol, what are you looking for? I've got a yard full of talent here, so whatever you want, I'm bound to have it.' He stuck his chest out in an effort to make himself look bigger and stronger.

'Um, I'm not exactly sure,' Sol replied. 'Just a friend, I think.'

'A friend is it, eh?' Alfred's eyes sparkled with anticipation. 'Then come and see Kite, she's as docile as they come.'

The mare had been there the longest, and no longer had the energy or the will to object to anything. She stood with her head hanging over the door in front of her, a slight widening of her air holes being her only acknowledgement of the two humans arriving before her.

'How old is she?' Sol asked.

'Barely ten, so lots of work left in her. Do you want to have a sit on her? She'll do anything you want.'

The young human rubbed a forelimb up and down Kite's neck, sorrow spilling out of him. 'No. Do you mind if I meet the rest of the horses on my own?'

'I mean, you can, but don't you want to know their age, background and the like?'

'Not for now, thanks.' Sol held the stare of his elder with a surety older than his years.

Disconcerted, Alfred stepped back, the top of his face crumpling. 'Okay, go ahead then. I'll just be in there, so give me a shout if there's anything you want to know, or if you want to ride any of them. Or, if you want, my son can sit on any of them you want to see ridden.'

Sol nodded. 'Will do.'

He approached each of our kind slowly, with sensitivity and compassion. Where most of them would flinch at the sight of

Chapter Thirteen

Alfred or Sean, they each greeted him from the place deep within themselves to which they had retreated from their situation. The energy of his heart enfolded them all, even as anger burned within him at their depressed yet fearful demeanour.

Old Betty made a noise deep within her throat as she sniffed his hand, his gentle energy reminding her of the elderly human whose transition to All That Is had resulted in her arrival at the yard. Her noise roused Lucky – who had retreated to the back of his stall and into himself following Sean's latest attempt to make him jump – from his exhausted, pain-ridden slumber.

He moved towards his stall door with trepidation, his fear of humans challenging the burst of hope surging through him at that which he sensed in the young male currently talking softly to Old Betty. This human differed from all those he had met in this incarnation. This one was open where the others were closed. He already had so much to teach, yet he was eager to learn. He knew not that it was balance for which he yearned, but he sought it anyway, driven by restlessness and frustration at the fact that his education regarding our kind had left him with more questions than answers. This was the human for whom he had been waiting since he was born.

Lucky lifted a tired forelimb and kicked the door to his stall. Sol startled at the noise and raised the top half of his face in surprise. He rubbed Old Betty's nose and then, leading with his shoulder so as to be as unthreatening as possible, sidled towards Lucky.

'Well, aren't you the noisy one?' He lifted the corners of his mouth. 'What is it you need?'

Lucky experienced a surge of strength at his sense that the inquiry was utterly genuine; the young human had every intention of attempting to meet his needs once he had identified them.

Lucky kicked the door harder. *I need you. You need me. Together we will move closer to that which we both crave.*

Sol stood in front of him, the corners of his mouth lifting higher. 'It's you, isn't it? You're the one who made me stop my car on the road outside, even though I must have driven past this vile place a hundred times.' He held out a forelimb to Lucky, who sniffed it all the way up to his head, soft noises emanating from his throat as he did so. The human tilted his head so that it rested against Lucky's nose. 'Why do I feel like I've been looking for you for years without even knowing it?'

Sol unbolted the door and stepped inside Lucky's stall, immediately moving away from him so as not to impose on his space uninvited. He tightened his mouth and blew out of it, making a quiet but shrill noise.

'So, they've whipped welts into you and spurred you until you bled,' he said, rage erupting out of him with such force that Lucky sidled away from him. The human breathed in and out deeply until his anger subsided. 'I'm sorry. Anger's the last thing you need to feel from me.' He held out his forelimb again until Lucky stepped closer. 'I'm just going to run my hands over you, okay? I'm taking you away from here regardless of what I find, but I just need to see if there's any other evidence of abuse.'

The energy of his heart accompanied each of his strokes of Lucky's body, soothing the pain and fear in each of his wounds; both those inflicted recently with intent and those inflicted historically in ignorance. He missed nothing but was unaware that it was the voice of his soul, rather than his hands, that told him of the stilted stride of Lucky's forelimbs due to the badly fitting implements he'd had strapped to his back, or of the soreness caused by the same.

'They used whips and spurs when they should have got you a healer and a saddler who knew what they were doing – and I bet

Chapter Thirteen

they didn't ask if you even wanted to be ridden first,' Sol said thoughtfully.

He and Lucky both jumped as Alfred's voice boomed into the stall. 'So, you like Lucky, eh? He's a superb choice. Just six years old, not done much, so a blank canvas you might say, and his breeding's to die for. Want to get him out?'

'He doesn't look very lucky to me,' Sol said, eyeing the wounds on Lucky's body. 'And by the look and feel of him, he's been made to do far more than should have been asked of a young horse.'

'Now look here…'

'I've already sent photos of his welts and spur wounds to my sister. If I don't call her within the next ten minutes, she'll not only forward them to the relevant authorities, she'll post them on social media along with this address. I'll give you a grand for this horse, and I'll take him within the hour.'

'He's worth ten times that. I have his papers, his sire…'

'Is irrelevant,' the young male said calmly.

'It's very relevant. His sire is a top showjumping stallion, and his dam won Badminton. There's no way you're taking him for a grand.'

'And yet he's ended up here, thrown away at just six years old and beaten to a pulp, presumably because you're determined to prove that you're the one who can do what others have failed to, and make him into what he was bred to be. He needs a vet and an osteopath, and probably months of remedial groundwork, before I can even think of seeing if he wants to be ridden. That's going to cost me a lot of money and time, so a grand is what I'll give you. Or…'

'You little shit, just who do you think you are?' Alfred said, the corner of his nose lifting as he spoke.

'Someone who doesn't need to worry about evidence of abuse

on his yard going viral on social media in…' Sol glanced at his forelimb. 'Seven minutes. I didn't just send photos of him to my sister, I sent them of all the horses here. There isn't a single one without an obvious sign of abuse, none of them have got anything to eat, and some of them haven't even got any water. Give me your bank details and I'll transfer the money and then call my sister to come and pick him up. Oh, and I'll take her too.' He tilted his head towards the wall on whose other side stood Old Betty. 'What is she, twenty-five? Thirty, even? And I bet you'll try to persuade some novice that she's fifteen. I'm also willing to bet you have her high on painkillers to mask the pain of her ringbone? She needs to live out her days in peace, and if I leave her here, that's not going to happen.'

'Two grand for the two of them,' Alfred said, his heart thumping fast and loud.

'One thousand two hundred for the two of them, and that's only because I need a receipt as proof that I'm their legal guardian. My sister's waiting for my call – you've now got five minutes.'

'Legal guardian? They're not kids, you arrogant little…'

'I never said they were. Do we have a deal?'

Life fluid surged to Alfred's face. He clenched and unclenched the digits of his forelimbs before finally saying. 'We have a deal. Transfer the money, take the horses, and never set foot on my yard again.'

Sol produced a small dark object from an opening in one of his garments and held it to his head. 'Sis? Yep, bring the lorry to the address I gave you. You sent the photos to Bridget? Cool, tell her to post them everywhere if she doesn't hear from me every ten minutes. Okay, take care, see you in a bit.' He tapped the object and said to Alfred, 'You got that? You lay one hand on me or any of the horses and Bridget will see this yard closed down.'

The elderly human clenched his teeth together, his face now a colour that was very unusual for his kind, and glared at Sol in silence.

'Good. We'll go to your office, shall we, and you can give me your account details, so I can transfer the money while you're writing me a receipt.'

Chapter Fourteen

To: info@horsewelfare.com
Subject: Abuse of horses by Alfred and Sean Bates
From: Hannah Grantham
Further to my phone call with Yasmin, please find below photos of all the horses at a yard owned and run by the above individuals. I understand you'll be sending officers to inspect the yard and horses this afternoon, and I would appreciate confirmation that this has occurred, and of the outcome of their visit.
Kind regards,
Hannah

BY THE TIME a large vessel rumbled onto the yard, Alfred had locked Sean into the office in order to prevent him assaulting the young human who was sitting calmly leaning back against Lucky's door, whilst Lucky breathed warm air onto the top of his head. All of our kind lifted their heads and made shrill noises in

Chapter Fourteen

anticipation of a new arrival – all except Kite, who stood as if vacant in both body and mind.

A young female jumped down from the front of the vessel and walked towards her brother, all the while staring at Kite. 'You good?' she said, glancing at him.

'Yep. Thanks for dropping everything and coming.'

She waved a forelimb at him. 'No problem, I can see why. What's wrong with that one?' She tilted her head towards Kite.

Sol let out a long breath. 'According to that arsehole, she's as quiet as, and will do anything you want.'

'And according to you?'

'She's very gentle and very sensitive. Her requests and protests have been met with shouting and beatings, so she's given up making them. I'd take her if I could, Hannah – I'd take them all – but you know I can only afford one comfortably, and I'm already taking two.'

'Learned helplessness,' Hannah said under her breath. 'Is she sound?'

Sol's eyes narrowed. 'You're thinking of having her?'

'Is she sound?' his sister repeated.

'I haven't seen her move. I can see if she's happy for me to run my hands over her and we can ask to see her led around, but she's bound to be on painkillers if she's got any problems, so she could have any number of them. I thought you said you'd never ride again after you finally got out of your cast, anyway?'

'I wasn't planning to. There's something about her though, isn't there? Or is it just me?'

Sol lifted the corners of his mouth. 'There's something about all of them, but where she's concerned, it's just you.' He lifted his forelimbs. 'Don't take that the wrong way, Han, it's a good thing. Did you call Horse Welfare?'

'Yep, they'll be here this afternoon, and Bridget's waiting for me to call and let her know we've left, then she'll give it half an hour and post your photos on social media.'

'Right then, let's have a look at Kite, get a deal done and be on our way, shall we?'

'I thought Bates senior was going to hit you, Sol,' Hannah said into the small object strapped in place by her forelimb, as she manoeuvred the vessel carrying Lucky, Old Betty and Kite out of the yard. 'How can you annoy people like that without worrying what might happen? I mean, I'm grateful to you for threatening him so he'd let me take Kite for five hundred quid, but how can you stay so calm while provoking so much rage?'

'Practice. Watch out for that car!' Sol shouted into the small dark object he had used to communicate with Hannah before her arrival at the yard.

'Do you want to drive?'

'I am driving. I'm right behind you, and I still saw that car first.'

'Drive the lorry, I meant, and I saw the damned car. What are we going to tell Mum and Dad when we pull into the yard with three horses?'

'That I've found the horse I never knew I was looking for, you've found a horse who's blasted your addiction to overthinking into outer space, and neither of us could have looked at ourselves in the mirror if we'd left Old Betty behind.'

'We're supposed to be running their livery business so they can retire, not filling their fields up with our own horses.'

'We'll pay for their keep, so what does it matter?'

'I s'ppose. You really think Kite will help me get my confidence back?'

Chapter Fourteen

'You already know she will. When she's ready though, Han. She'll help you, but it needs to be on her terms.'

'That should make me nervous, but it doesn't. Isn't that weird?'

'For a control freak like you, yes, but good weird. Are they all okay in the back?'

'Yep, they're travelling as quietly as they loaded. See you at home?'

'See you at home.'

'You'll want to be getting on that horse soon. Put any more condition on him, and he'll be a bit much.'

Sol took a long, deep breath and then slowly exhaled his irritation before turning away from Lucky, with whom he had been enjoying a mutual groom, to face one of those who believed she owned one of our kind. 'A bit much for who?' he asked her.

'Well, for you! You don't want him having too much to say for himself and having you off in front of your liveries, do you?'

Sol lifted the corners of his mouth and showed his teeth even though he felt like doing neither. 'I know you have your ways of doing things, Francis, but I don't think Lucky can ever have too much to say for himself. If he's happy to be ridden and I don't prove up to the task and fall off him, then I'll be thinking about what I can do better, rather than worrying what my liveries think – no disrespect.'

The middle-aged human shook her head. 'Tsk, tsk, if he's happy to be ridden? That's what he's here for, isn't it? These horses cost too much to keep just to be field ornaments. What your parents must have thought when you turned up with these three, I can only imagine.' She waved a forelimb at where Lucky was now grazing alongside Kite and Old Betty, then stared at Sol, the top half of her face lifted in anticipation of a response.

'Well, I'd better get back to it,' Sol said, waving a grooming implement. 'I've got all the mucking out to do once I've spent some quality time with my boy.'

Francis wandered off, shaking her head, only to be replaced by another human on her way back to the yard after releasing her partner onto an area of grass beside the one shared by Lucky, Kite and Old Betty. This female was younger and moved with an expectation of being stared at by other humans.

'Well, they're all looking a lot better than when they got here,' she said. 'What are you going to do with them?'

Sol forced his mouth back into the expression that gave other humans the impression he was pleased to see them. He scratched Lucky's back, and his partner immediately stopped eating and rubbed Sol's shoulder with the end of his nose. 'We don't have any plans. I think Betty just wants to mooch around out here with the other horses, but we'll see what Lucky and Kite feel up to once the osteopath is happy with them.

The young female nodded approvingly. 'You'll be wanting those shoes off them, won't you? And you'll be wanting to go bitless. I'm not sure how Hannah will cope with that now that she's so nervous though. I know a fantastic saddler who'll come out when their backs are sorted, and I'll give you the number of my trainer. He's into doing everything naturally; he's a total breath of fresh air.'

Sol allowed her to talk herself out without replying, then waved his grooming implement in a relieved farewell when she announced that she couldn't stand around talking all day.

He moved the implement along Lucky's back in long strokes and soon lost himself in the sense of wellbeing emanating from his partner. The heat provider soothed them both with warm,

Chapter Fourteen

gentle rays, and the feathered fliers swooped around them, singing their happiness as they removed biters from the air. Despite Sol's intention to return to the yard in order to fulfil his duties, he couldn't bring himself to end his time with his friend.

As a youngster, he had avoided all the group activities involving our kind in which his sister had taken part, preferring instead to be alone with his partner of the time. When his parents had insisted he receive education into young adulthood, he had chosen to study our kind with those deemed experts on the subject. While he had enjoyed his learning, he felt stifled by the idea that there was a "correct" way to be around us, interact with us, and ride us. He finished his education with the highest level of approval from his teachers, but he never spoke about his knowledge and training, for he felt it was far from complete.

Whenever he was with those of our kind, he felt as if he were learning that which had been missing from his formal education, even if he often couldn't organise what he had learnt into the words that humans found so beneficial.

The longer he spent working his way around Lucky's body, removing hard pieces of earth from his coat, separating the hairs of his mane and tail so that they were more effective at flicking away biters, and massaging him in places where soreness was being replaced by health, the more sure he was of what Lucky wanted; not because he thought about it and came to a conclusion, but because he knew in the way that the horses know.

Lucky wanted to be ridden. He wanted to explore ways of using his body that he wouldn't without the stimulation of a rider. He wanted to explore how his body could interact with that of a human in such a way that both of them could clear aspects of their past and move closer to balance. He wanted a connection with Sol that would be a living embodiment of oneness, so that Sol could complete the learning for which he yearned, and they could both enter their next incarnation together primed for the parts they would be required to play.

Sol was suddenly aware, through Lucky's awareness of our celebration of their partnership, of the rest of us who would share their mission. He knew not what it was that he felt, exactly, only that in following his own path through his life with our kind, he had stumbled across something far larger than that for which he had thought he was searching. His strokes became shorter and eventually stopped as he explored that which he knew.

When Hannah came to find him, he was sitting on the ground, picking stalks of grass whilst Lucky, Kite and Old Betty did likewise around him.

'Sol? What is it? Are you okay?' She bent her body in order to fit between the planks of the fence and hurried to his side. 'Sol?'

When he lifted the corners of his mouth and showed his teeth this time, it was a genuine expression of how he was feeling. 'I'm better than okay. It's time; Lucky wants to be ridden. Kite's ready for you too, by the way. She's here for you for the same reason Lucky's here for me. And when we've done everything we already know how to do, we'll be ready for what will come next.'

'What do you mean? What will come next? I'm not aiming for the national championships again after what happened last time. I pushed myself and Cain too hard, we had a terrible fall, and now he's dead and I'm barely living.' Hannah's breath came out hard and fast, as if she had been running at full speed for some time.

Sol got to his feet and took her forelimbs in his. 'All you need to think about, or better still, not think about, is how it feels to be with Kite. She's got you, Han. Come on over here and give her a scratch. Don't think about anything other than finding today's favourite scratchy spot. When you've found it, keep focusing on that and nothing else until you know what you know.'

'What do you mean?'

Chapter Fourteen

'You'll know when you know it. You can do this, Han. You wouldn't have been so adamant about bringing Kite home if you couldn't. I'm going to do the mucking out, then I'm going to put a bridle together and look out some saddles to try on Lucky. I think starting with what he already knows is the best way to go, then he can let me know if he wants something different. See you in a bit.'

When he reached the fence, having left Hannah running her hands over a delighted Kite, yet another female was waiting for him. 'Did I just hear you say you're going to ride Lucky? And in a bridle and saddle, no less? You shouldn't feel you have to ride him just because of what everyone thinks, you know. Horses weren't made to be ridden, and they certainly don't like wearing bridles and saddles.'

'How do you know, have you asked them all?' Sol said, attempting to keep weariness and frustration out of his voice.

'Well, no, but I've been reading this book that says…'

'I'm far more interested in what my horse says,' Sol interrupted, walking faster to try to outpace the young female.

'What do you mean? He can't talk.'

'He doesn't communicate in the way we do but that doesn't mean he can't let me know what he wants, and I fully intend to ask him, every step of the way.'

'Ask him?'

'Yes. He's the only one who knows what's important to him and how he wants to go about living his life. Everything else is just noise.'

'But my book says that horses…'

Sol allowed her voice to drift around him as she explained what horses needed, and excused himself from her company as soon as they reached the yard.

∞

Sol went on to become a much sought after trainer in the ways of our kind – not because he chose teaching as a profession, but because the bond he shared with Lucky was so strong as to be obvious to those around them. The affection they had for one another, their mutual understanding and their ability to move together in complete harmony had Sol and Hannah's liveries stopping to watch them whenever they were together, whether Sol was riding Lucky or not. They asked for his help in achieving the same degree of trust and co-operation with their partners, and so did their friends, and their friends' friends.

With Sol and Kite's help, Hannah regained her confidence as a rider, and the pair were almost as harmonious to watch as Sol and Lucky. But Hannah would only ever ride Kite; there was only so far that she was willing to go in confronting the fear of failure that had remained with her after she pushed herself and her previous partner to catastrophe. She refused Sol's repeated requests for her and Kite to act as a demonstration partnership when he was lecturing to large audiences, and only ever rode once their liveries had gone home.

Kite was content with the progress Hannah made, and the bond they developed in the process. It carried them into their current incarnation as Holly and Serene, and remained strong enough that it would give them the foundation from which they would flourish under the influence of Walks A Straight Path. She and I would need to be stronger in our encouragement of the two gentle souls than Sol had been though.

As a result of all he achieved with Lucky's help, Sol had little left to do on the physical plane before his need to incarnate would be no more, but his bond with his partner had carried him into their current incarnation as Shann and Spider in order to support those of us who were less advanced and had more of a burden to clear.

Spider was currently practising emphasising the dominant aspects of his beloved partner's personality so that he was becoming a bigger version of himself. While the veil that Shann's soul had pulled down when incarnating into a human body was thick enough to keep the truth of existence from him, it was thinner than most, to the extent that Shann found it impossible to take life seriously. His sense of fun and mischief was amplified by Spider, and the two of them lifted those around them out of the human tendency to worry, to the place of humour and light-heartedness from which they were much better able to learn.

I allowed Spider and Serene's experience to mould me further; Walks A Straight Path and I would magnify one another's strengths and be compelling enough examples to those around us that they couldn't help but be moved to do as we did.

I remembered back to when we had done it before; when Senses Balance had declared with such courage and sincerity his lack of fear at being forced to ride towards his death in a senseless war, moving four nearby souls to feel likewise and embrace their own end. All four of them had been drawn to us on our return to All That Is and would be drawn to us again when we reappeared in their lives this time around. Marvel, Vickery, Aleks and Sonja may not have been aware that they were waiting for Walks A Straight Path to create the ripple through their current incarnation that would draw them inexorably to its source, but their Bond-Partners knew. The Horses Of The New Dawn who were now incarnate as Broad, Verve, Nexus and Bright waited for my Bond-Partner as surely as they did me, and as they sensed the touch of my mind upon theirs, each experienced a surge of anticipation.

Tentatively, I led them to Walks A Straight Path so that they would be aware of her progress. I found her straining so hard to conjure a complex ailment in her mind, with the intention of ascertaining whether a particular herb would cure it, that she wasn't capable of being aware of anything else. For once, I allowed myself to linger close to her without concern that she would take hold of my mind and follow it before time, so that I could sense all she now was.

Whilst she had been born a strong and wilful character, she was now growing in confidence with every cycle of light and darkness as a result of her success in gathering and assimilating the knowledge and skill that would aid us once we bonded. Where her single-mindedness had been deemed a failing by her herd and her educators when she was younger, it was now considered an advantage as she surpassed most of those who had gone before her in her field of healing. She had only a little more maturing to do before our mission could begin. I rejoiced in that knowledge, to the extent that I was forced to pull away from her lest she sense me. I resolved to remain patient until the time came for my soul to call to hers.

It would be another full cycle of the earth providing its myriad of responses to the position of the heat provider before that came to pass.

When it finally did, the heat provider had long since passed its highest point above us for the fifth time in my life, so that its rays now brushed across us rather than pounding down upon us, and the shade providers were rapidly dropping their nutrition. I was grazing peacefully alongside my dam when a sudden and definite shift occurred both within me and Walks A Straight Path. Apart, whilst inexorably together, we had finally reached a point where we had accumulated the knowledge, strength and confidence we would need, whilst retaining the openness and flexibility of our youth.

My soul sang so loudly with joy that I was sure it must be audible. We were ready.

Chapter Fifteen

I'm so enjoying being allowed to treat Nerys's patients! I feel proud of myself every time I diagnose their condition correctly and prescribe the herbs that I know will help. Nerys is always there observing, and I love it when she tilts her head forward a bit, so that only I notice, to let me know I've got the dosage right. I wonder if it's wrong though, that the bit I enjoy most about my apprenticeship is being out and about by myself, finding new herbs and seeing how I can use them? I think it's because I only wanted to be a Herbalist so I can help my horse. I'm nearly qualified now, so I hope she tugs me soon. Everything I've done has been for her, and I've waited so long, I don't think I can bear to wait much longer.

Diary of Amarilla Nixon, aged 16

MY HERD SENSED the shift in me, and I felt their immediate acceptance that I would leave them. They were withdrawing their energy from me even as I allowed my mind to reach along the thread connecting me and Walks A Straight Path.

She was studying the energy vibration of a herb that was new to her and for which in time she would find an application… but that time was not now. I at last allowed my mind to touch hers and our souls to reaffirm our bond.

I sensed her recognition followed by her delight, but then all of a sudden, something didn't feel right. Instead of merely embracing the pull of my mind upon hers and preparing herself to follow it to where we would meet, Walks A Straight Path hurled herself along our thread and into my body, forcing her own body to abandon her endeavour and move at full speed towards me in a desperate attempt not to lose touch with her mind.

That wasn't how it should be; she needed her mind to ensure the survival of her own body, not lodge itself within mine. She wasn't safe.

I left my herd at a run. Many of my kind startled and stared around themselves, ears flickering and noses drawing in the surrounding scents, wondering from whence the threat was coming that had made me run without warning. Others stood rigid, watching my dam for her reaction. She rested a hind limb as she watched me heading towards the destiny I was born to fulfil. The energy of her heart followed me for a time, grieving for me even as it reassured me that I had the skills and strength I needed in order to survive without her. When it followed me no more, I grieved too – but not for long. The energy of my heart may have been strong enough to reassure my entire herd when necessary, but in her current predicament, Walks A Straight Path needed it in its entirety.

Where I had been aware of, and learnt from, the other Horses Of The New Dawn as part of my preparation for my time with Walks A Straight Path, she had grown up completely isolated from the humans who had the knowledge and experience to educate and support a mind like hers. Her response to the pull of my mind on hers was unlike any other human who had been called to bond with one of our kind, and without assistance, her loss of mind would become permanent. She would be with me as we had planned, but in mind and soul only; we needed her to be firmly rooted in her body so that she was with me in that too, but she was already leaving it behind. As fast as she was running towards me, she was too far away to be able to catch up with her mind before it would detach from her.

When she collapsed and fell into an exhausted slumber, I too ceased my frantic journey. Whilst nourishing my body, I tried without success to push her mind back to where her injured, neglected body lay. When she woke and resumed her pursuit of both me and her mind, I tried again repeatedly, hoping she would sense that which I was trying to do and allow me to push her back into herself. But she resisted; with every push against her mind, she launched it even harder back to me, so desperate was she to maintain the level of connection for which she had waited so long, and so convinced that all would be well once she was with me.

Thankfully, when she collapsed again, she found herself close to some nutrition, for which her body was now desperate. I relaxed a little at her body's relief as she tended to its needs, and as a result, I focused more on my own surroundings. I was relatively safe as I raced across open ground, and well provided for by bountiful grass and plentiful bodies of water, but even so, I missed my dam and my herd. My mind flew back to Walks A Straight Path. She was my herd now, so long as she survived long enough for me to reach her.

When she slept, I rested by some shade providers that stood tall in the otherwise flat landscape, whilst still trying to push the bulk of her mind back to her, where it belonged – but in vain.

During the next few cycles of light and darkness, Walks A Straight Path lived according to her name; she forced her steadily weakening, injured body in my direction regardless of its needs or anything that stood in its way. She took in sustenance when she happened upon it, but other than that, her sole focus was on finding me, regardless of the threat to her survival. I found myself becoming ever more frustrated and frantic at my failure to push her back into herself so that she would be capable of taking a more balanced approach towards her journey to meet me.

Though I diverted from my path occasionally in order to find water or somewhere to rest, I expended ever more of myself in my effort to reach her and ensure her survival, to the point where I needed help myself – and The Horses Of The New Dawn provided it. All except she who would be Flame had experience of leaving their herds in order to find their Bond-Partner, and all knew how it was to be alone and vulnerable for the first time. They gave me their energy so that I could travel faster and further each day. They employed my senses to monitor my surroundings so that I could sleep safe in the knowledge that they would rouse me should danger approach. They bolstered my sense of myself as a contributor to our joint mission and as such, my confidence that I would reach Walks A Straight Path before her body failed – that together, we would still succeed.

It wasn't enough. Walks A Straight Path's body was failing faster than I could travel to find her. I now needed the strength of Oak not only to fortify myself, but to work through his Bond-Partner and save Walks A Straight Path. He was the closest of us to her in proximity, and the instant he sensed my request, he relayed it to Rowena.

Relieved as I was to sense the two of them immediately hastening towards Walks A Straight Path, I continued my race towards her as well as my attempts to push the majority of her

Chapter Fifteen

mind back to its proper place of residence. But it was so strong. Even as her body became more frail, her mind retained its determination to sit within mine until she found me. It was only when her legs crumpled and she was overcome by a swirling sensation in her head before losing awareness of herself and her environment, that I was finally able to overcome her desire to be with me in her entirety and reacquaint her mind with her body.

While I was concerned that the strength of her mind was diminished now that she was unconscious rather than merely asleep, I was relieved at the sense of rightness emanating from our bond now that she was no longer attempting to force it to be somewhere it was never intended to be. And while I was concerned about the condition of her body, I took comfort from the rapidly increasing nearness of Oak and his Bond-Partner to her. The two of them were firmly rooted in both the physical reality and in their bond, and would be a much needed source of stability for my beloved soulmate.

I was aware the instant they found her. I saw her through Oak's eyes as he walked towards her prone body, and I felt the weight of her as Rowena draped her across his back. She was frail, but she was alive. Her mind was unconscious, but it was where it should be, and I would use all my strength to ensure it remained there. Now that she was with Oak, she would survive.

I continued to move steadily towards her through the light and then the darkness, calm and determined now where I had been agitated and concerned. I leant firmly against her mind in order to prevent her hurling it into me again, so that in her brief spells of wakefulness, she was aware of me as a part of her existence rather than the majority of it. Nevertheless, her mind quested for me whilst she was both awake and asleep; I may have managed to rebalance our bond, but that did not affect her desperation and determination to know how I was, where I was or when we would meet.

I was doing all I could for now; once we were together, I would encourage our partnership towards one that was more balanced.

I sensed Walks A Straight Path's upset at her body's condition when she finally noticed how she had abused it. An elderly male human spoke gently to her.

'Right, my dear, up you get. There's a nice hot bath waiting for you upstairs, and I've a stew on that should be ready by the time you've finished. I'm Adam, by the way.'

I sensed who he was to Rowena and Oak and then knew him in his entirety. He Who Is Peace. As was his wont, he was infusing Walks A Straight Path with the attribute he had worked so hard to attain during his time with his Bond-Partner, and she began to relax under his care.

It was only after he had ensured that she tended to all her body's needs, including a long sleep, that he and Rowena helped her to understand her behaviour since I called her to me. As a result, I was relieved not to have to lean so hard against her mind to keep it where it was. At last, she was with those who would educate and support her as the other Horses Of The New Dawn had done for me.

They sensed my relief and my proximity to Walks A Straight Path. Their anticipation of our now imminent meeting lifted us all to revel where we could do so without limit, at our plans arriving at the brink of fruition. We swooped and spun as one in the grey of All That Is, celebrating our connection, our recognition of our joint purpose and our intended mission, as we

Chapter Fifteen

had done so often before. This time though, we exulted in the fact that finally, Walks A Straight Path and I would be joining the rest.

By the time we had finished expressing our merriment and once more focused the majority of ourselves in our physicality, Walks A Straight Path had left He Who Is Peace, Oak and Rowena and was once more making her way towards me. I sensed her excitement, but it was tempered now by the realisation that she needed to take far better care of herself than she had when leaving her home and herd.

I was gladdened when she halted her journey in order to nourish her body, even if she did surrender to her excitement at sensing my approval and immediately resume her journey.

I'm coming. Unlike other bonded humans, Walks A Straight Path was not only immediately comfortable conversing with me using her mind, but didn't wait to be with me in body, or for me to initiate communication before doing so. She didn't yet know that most of the communication she intended to have with me would be unnecessary, but she would learn.

When I sensed she was near, I halted on the side of the tall mound of earth whose opposite sides she and I had been climbing, where there was grass that I found to be highly agreeable. Now that we had both come so far and were so close, there was no rush.

Though the heat provider was low in the sky when her gaze finally landed upon me, there was sufficient light to meet her eyes with mine. It was as though the world exploded for an instant; our souls exulted, our minds settled into our bond as if the madness of the recent cycles of light and darkness had never occurred, and our bodies regarded one other with awe and satisfaction – the perfect match to dance the adventure we had planned.

You are here. I put my overwhelming sense of rightness into my thought before lowering my head back down to the grass.

It wasn't enough for her. She watched me in consternation for a while and then replied, *You're still grazing.*

Whilst I sensed that she expected a response, she had asked no question.

I've arrived, I've found you, so why are you still grazing? she asked.

I am hungry. I stated the obvious in order to satisfy her rising confusion. I would not be making a habit of it.

Oh. She accepted my explanation only because she knew not what else to do. She felt a need to learn everything about me – why I had chosen her, why she had been aware of me since she was so young, and what I intended to teach her. She had not realised that I was already teaching her.

She fidgeted with her belongings until the heat provider had disappeared, taking most of its light with it. Her body was announcing its needs, but she was increasingly being consumed by a rage that obliterated her awareness of it.

When she got to her feet, I raised my head to observe her with my eyes as well as my mind and soul. She made herself taller and filled her steps towards me with fury, the like of which I had so far not encountered in this incarnation. My body responded to hers, as it always would. I spun around and fled from her until her wrath changed to confusion and then concern. I stopped and turned to face her, the fear that had fuelled my body's instinct having been discharged.

Walks A Straight Path's anger returned. 'Why are you ignoring me?' Her first use of her voice in my presence was much louder than I sensed was usual for her. 'Don't you know how far I have come, what I've been through, to find you? And then you just carry on grazing as if I weren't here?'

I gathered together our past, our present and our future – everything she was to me – and enfolded her with it along with the

Chapter Fifteen

energy of my heart. *You are here. I am here. Everything is as it should be.*

Walks A Straight Path drew my counsel into the depths of her soul and relaxed. She tended to her body's needs and then sat watching me while I did likewise. When I eventually lay down beside her, she moved closer and curled up between my limbs, her back to my belly. Our souls hummed with joy as they interwove, entwining so tightly with one another that we could never exist apart again. I had never felt so content.

We would rest and then when light replaced darkness, we would make our way to The Gathering.

The Horses Of The New Dawn were waiting.

Books by Lynn Mann

The Horses Know Trilogy
The Horses Know
The Horses Rejoice
The Horses Return

Sequels to The Horses Know Trilogy
Horses Forever
The Forgotten Horses
The Way Of The Horse

Origins of The Horses Know Trilogy
The Horses Unite
The Horses Of The New Dawn

Prequels to The Horses Know Trilogy
An Element Of Risk (Devlin's story)
In Search Of Peace (Adam's story)
The Strength Of Oak (Rowena's story)
A Reason To Be Noble (Quinta's story)

Companion Stories to The Horses Know Trilogy
From A Spark Comes A Flame
Tales Of The Horse-Bonded (Short Story Collection)
Tales Of The Horse-Bonded will take you on a journey into the lives of some of your favourite characters from *The Horses Know Trilogy*. The book is available for purchase in paperback and hardback, but is also available to download for free. To find out more, visit www.lynnmann.co.uk.

A regularly updated book list can be found at
www.lynnmann.co.uk/booklist
Use the QR code below for easy access:

'

Did you enjoy *The Horses Of The New Dawn*?
I'd be extremely grateful if you could spare a few minutes
to leave a review where you purchased your copy.
Reviews really do help my books to reach a wider audience,
which means that I can keep on writing!
Thank you very much.

I love to hear from you!
Get in touch and receive news of future releases at the following:

www.lynnmann.co.uk

www.facebook.com/lynnmann.author

Acknowledgments

Thank you, lovely readers, for reading this last book in *The Horses Know* series. Having had it in my head for a while that I wanted to write a story to link *The Horses Unite* to *The Horses Know,* so that the eight books in the main series form a circle, I'm delighted to have finally done it!

I won't lie, the story was a challenge to write, as I wanted to tell it from Infinity's point of view but without coming across as speaking for the horses, or humanising them. It was also a delight to write, because in narrating from Infinity's point of view, I had her in my head with me for weeks on end, which I absolutely loved.

My enormous gratitude goes, as always, to my editorial team, whose help has been even more necessary and valued than usual due to brain fog clogging my thought process – Fern Sherry, Caroline Macintosh and Cindy Nye, you are all total legends.

Huge thanks also to Jon Morris of MoPhoto for the use of his photos of Pie on the cover and the first pages of each chapter, and to Amanda Horan for her fabulous cover design.

My home team of Darren and Ivy Mann were a wonderful and hugely appreciated source of calm support as I struggled to wrestle my brain into gear.

My final thanks go to the horse without whom none of my books would have been written – Pie, your influence on me is incalculable, cherished and everlasting.

www.ingramcontent.com/pod-product-compliance
Lightning Source LLC
Chambersburg PA
CBHW061209070526
44583CB00025B/3178